CONQUERING
Content Vocabulary

A hands-on approach
to learning academic vocabulary

Chelsea Tornetto

■SCHOLASTIC

New York • Toronto • London • Auckland • Sydney
Mexico City • New Delhi • Hong Kong • Buenos Aires

Dedication

To my parents and grandparents, for building up my confidence as a writer from a young age and for always being proud and supportive of my career as an educator.

To Mr. Osman, for his unfailing wit and wisdom and for inspiring me to do big things; and to Mrs. Fahey, for never settling for less than the perfect "power paragraph!"

To my husband and best friend, Mike. Coming home and "talking school" with you is better than any professional development I could attend. Thank you for always pushing me past my self-doubt . . . and for watching the kids while I run off to Panera to write!

To Rachel Glisson, for all the time you spent reading and editing my first draft to make it "shine!"

To Maria Chang, for picking my proposal out of the pile and for introducing me to the world of publishing.

To my awesome colleagues, past and present, at Jackson R2 Schools. I feel so blessed to live and work in a district that encourages innovation and improvement and where the teachers truly care about student success—not just on a test—but in life!

Editor: Maria L. Chang
Cover design by Tannaz Fassihi
Interior design by Abby Dening

ISBN: 978-1-338-17434-2
Copyright © 2018 by Chelsea Tornetto
All rights reserved.
Printed in the U.S.A.
First printing, January 2018.

1 2 3 4 5 6 7 8 9 10   40   25 24 23 22 21 20 19 18

Contents

The Go-To in Your Tool Belt

With more than a decade of teaching experience under my belt, I've seen my share of education trends come and go. In our district, we call it the "Flavor of the Month"—the never-ending cycle of new "best practices," each of which will supposedly turn even the most combative student into an eager lover of learning and make everything we've been doing in our classrooms for years obsolete.

Here's pretty much how it goes . . .

You show up for a Professional Development (PD) day, energized and excited about learning new ways to impart knowledge to young minds . . . and, let's face it, really looking forward to leaving the building for a whole hour and eating lunch at an actual restaurant! Mexican, anyone?

You settle in for the morning, and after you've "gotten to know" your neighbor (whom you've taught with for years) through an icebreaker that resembles an awkward adult version of musical chairs, the real presentation begins.

Five mini–candy bars and several bathroom breaks later, you are so overwhelmed with information—most of which was presented to you in the form of a 76-slide PowerPoint˚ presentation—that your brain can barely remember what grade you teach, let alone how any of the strategies presented could be used in your classroom. Your butt hurts from sitting, your hand hurts from doodling (I mean, taking notes), and worst of all, your ego hurts a little (okay, maybe a lot) because according to the presenter, every tried-and-true strategy you've ever used is crap. You make it through the rest of the morning and leave for that much anticipated lunch break, blinking as your tired eyes adjust to the sunlight, feeling like a failure. And not all that excited about developing yourself professionally.

Sound familiar?

When I was a new teacher, days like these could literally bring me to tears. I felt like I had to change everything about the way I taught by the next school day to be considered a good teacher. Now that I'm more experienced, I still feel a bit anxious when PD days roll around, but now I know that the best way to improve my instruction is not to adopt every new trend that comes along. Nor is it to drown your sorrows in margaritas at that Mexican restaurant! Instead, I've learned to choose only the best strategies—the ones that really work for ME—from each Professional Development day and add them to my teacher tool belt, so to speak.

In construction, the purpose of a tool belt is to keep the tools used most often within easy reach. Construction workers don't carry around every single tool they own in their belts; they carry only the ones they know are going to come in handy on a regular basis. Your "teacher tool belt" should work the same way. Sure, you might need that "parts of a cell" role-playing activity someday, but it isn't something you are going to use on a daily, or even weekly, basis. No need to carry it around in that overtasked brain of yours; that's what filing cabinets are for! Well, that and hiding the good candy from students . . .

Or, think of it like shopping! You don't go out and buy every new high-fashion trend that hits the stores, do you? You pick and choose the ones that fit your own personal style. Good teachers do this naturally (with teaching strategies . . . not always with fashion). We try something new, and if as we're doing it we can feel that the strategy "fits" our teaching style, matches the goals we have for our students and our districts, and works, then we keep it. We do it again the following week. We tell our colleagues about it in the hall between classes. We find ourselves modifying it on the fly and making it better, because we've internalized it and made it our own. It becomes a go-to tool.

Vocabulary Connection Cards is one of those tools for me. I learned the basic strategy of a concept sort years ago. But the minute I tried it in my own room, it became mine. Over the past years I've added to it, modified it, improved upon it, and adapted it until it became Vocabulary Connection Cards—and a regular part of my teaching routine.

This book doesn't claim to offer a new, groundbreaking strategy, but instead simply seeks to present a collection of the most effective, teacher-tested ways to use concept sorts in your classroom. By the time you finish reading, I hope to have demonstrated how this versatile tool can enrich your content-area vocabulary lessons and how it can be integrated with other forms of instruction to make your life easier and your students smarter. I tried to tailor the ideas for middle- and upper-grade non-ELA teachers, who are struggling to fit vocabulary into an already bulging curriculum, by highlighting how this strategy could be used more often and more effectively in your classroom in a way that does not insult what you currently do.

The first two chapters in this book give a clear explanation of what Vocabulary Connection Cards are and who they're designed for, as well as step-by-step instructions on how best to use them. I then outline the Three Stages of Vocabulary Instruction, including strategies for using Connection Cards at each stage. You'll also find tips on how to utilize these cards to boost students' writing, as well as ideas for strengthening the home-school connection. Finally, I provide reproducible sample sets of Vocabulary Connection Cards for math, science, and social studies that you can use immediately and adapt or build upon.

As with all professional development, I don't expect every person who reads this book to fall in love with this strategy. It will work for some and not for others. But I do believe that it is a simple and reliable way to increase and deepen student learning that can be integrated into any teacher's current teaching style—and that won't run you ragged in the process.

And that's the kind of tool every teacher should have in his or her tool belt!

Chapter One

What Are Vocabulary Connection Cards?

Vocabulary Connection Cards are made up of approximately 25 to 35 keywords from any particular unit of study, written on individual cards, and used to facilitate student discussion and the creation of mental connections between those keywords. They are a visual, auditory, and kinesthetic approach to learning the deeper meaning behind content-related vocabulary—so students don't just "get" the definition, they actually understand the meaning.

They Are for Content Area Teachers

The strategies provided are intended for teachers outside the English Language Arts curriculum. Why not ELA, you ask? Well . . .

When I started teaching, I taught six sections of 7th grade world geography, and I found myself running into the same problem over and over again. We would be in the middle of a great class discussion. You know, the kind where your teacher-spidey-senses are tingling, the kids are itching to contribute genuinely intelligent comments, and at the back of your mind you are thinking, "I LOVE TEACHING!" and "Why can't an administrator walk in right now?" When suddenly, a hand would shoot up.

"What does that mean?"

Sometimes it would be a new word, like *Sunni* or *communism*. But often it would be a more widely applicable word, like *globalization*. Either way, conversation would stop so I could define the word and give the context of its meaning, before we could get back to business.

Ironically, it wasn't until I was asked to teach language arts for half my day that I was able to dissect the problem I'd been having in world geography. My language arts colleagues were constantly talking about vocabulary—how to teach it, when to teach it, but mostly, which words to teach. Sometimes they would choose to teach difficult words that were found in a class reading piece, frequently misspelled words, or words with common roots, prefixes, or suffixes. Other times they would simply choose interesting words or words they thought would improve students' creativity in writing. Ultimately, the reason for choosing each word was not all that important, so long as new, grade-appropriate words were being taught.

Two things about this blew my mind: First, the idea that they were making time in the curriculum just to teach vocabulary was a little bit mind-boggling. In social studies, I had so much content to cover in a year that the idea of taking even part of a lesson just to teach the meanings of words my students were puzzled by seemed a somewhat frivolous waste of time. Second, I couldn't quite wrap my brain around the idea that it really didn't matter what words they taught in language arts! In social studies, there are very specific words students need to know—words that often aren't found in a standard dictionary.

Teaching both courses every day led me to engage in a very natural process of comparing and contrasting and transferring teaching strategies from one to the other. And as I did, I came to a rather obvious conclusion—**teaching vocabulary in the content areas is vastly different from teaching vocabulary in a language arts setting, and therefore requires a different approach.** I know . . . duh, right?

In language arts, when we say we are teaching vocabulary, we are actually teaching a skill. The purpose of teaching vocabulary in an ELA classroom is to help students learn how to identify any words they don't know as they read. We teach them to recognize roots, prefixes, and suffixes, use context clues, and so on . . . you know the drill. Mastering those strategies makes reading comprehension easier overall. But precisely which vocabulary words we use to teach them this skill is not super important. Sure, common sense dictates that we choose words that are academic and are bound to show up in assessments and other courses, but otherwise, whatever words we think are important work great! Just teach students as many words as we can in a year.

In social studies, science, or math, the purpose is much different. In these classrooms, teachers teach a very specific set of vocabulary words not as a skill, but as content. Students don't just need to be able to use the word in a sentence or identify its meaning using context clues, they need to own it! Really understanding a word's meaning isn't going to simply make the reading piece easier to comprehend; really understanding its meaning is the objective! In content-area classrooms, a student may be able to use the word in a sentence, write out its definition, and correctly complete a matching quiz—and still not meet that objective.

So what's a frustrated social studies teacher to do? I first turned to my world geography textbook for guidance. But the vocabulary "activities" I found there looked something like the example at right.

VOCABULARY

Match each word in the first column with its definition in the second column.

WORD	DEFINITION
1. aqueduct	a. the practice and skill of public speaking
2. fresco	b. thousands of tiny colored stone cubes set in plaster to create a picture or design
3. parable	c. a painting done on plaster walls
4. barbarian	d. a system of government in which there are four rulers
5. oratory	e. a member of a tribe outside the empire
6. bas-relief	f. a simple story told to make a moral point
7. tetrarchy	g. a stone channel that carries water
8. mosaic	h. a sculpture with figures raised against a flat background

(Hiebert, 2016)

I quickly found that my kids could get a perfect score on quizzes like these and still not be able to use a word correctly in a sentence. So I moved on to the following graphic organizer below:

Definition:	Characteristics:
Examples:	Non-Examples:

This type of four-square graphic organizer (modified from the Frayer Model, developed by Dorothy Frayer and her colleagues at the University of Wisconsin in 1969) is certainly a step up from the mind-numbing practice of copying and memorizing definitions from the glossary, which I had been subjected to in elementary school.

But there were several problems.

First, the Frayer Model just doesn't work for some super content-specific terms that we content-area teachers need to cover. For instance, what is a non-example of *Mesopotamia*? Or *photosynthesis*? Or *factors*? What are the characteristics of *veto*? Or *variables*? Can you give me an example of *Continental Congress*? The Frayer Model is fabulous for some words, but just doesn't work for many others and often leads to a line of students at my desk, whining, "I don't get it." Ugh.

In addition, I found that even though my students could complete the graphic organizer correctly and could almost always identify the correct definitions on a quiz, they often struggled or downright flopped when I asked them to put that definition in their own words or explain it with regard to the topic we were discussing in class. They were memorizing definitions instead of mastering concepts. And I was losing time.

No offense, Frayer, but four-squares take FOREVER.

Finally, I broke down and did something no self-respecting woman ever does unless she is truly stumped . . . I asked my husband! Actually, I'm very lucky to be married to a guy who is not only a teacher like me, but who is a great sounding board for ideas and a great inspiration when it comes to instruction. He teaches high school–level advanced placement history courses, but has experience with special-education integration, middle school, and just about everything in between.

So I asked him, "How do you teach vocabulary?"

He replied, "I don't know. I mean, when I'm lecturing about the material and a word comes up that they don't know, I tell them what it means. I guess I just explain each word as I come to it, and then move on. Hopefully, we use each word enough in class that they remember it." He paused, shook his head, and said defensively, "I don't have time to teach vocabulary. I have seniors. I have too much content to teach—way more than you."

Cue two-hour argument about whose job is harder.

In all seriousness, though, I found that everyone I talked to outside of an ELA classroom had similar responses. We have too much to teach! We just don't have time! If I take the time to teach straight vocabulary, I have to cut something out.

But the more I thought about it, the more I began to believe that my fellow social studies teachers and I were making a mistake by thinking we should ever teach "straight vocabulary" anyway. True, we didn't have time (or the desire) to make our students take matching quizzes or use each word in complete, grammatically correct sentences, or complete a bazillion four-squares. But even if we did, is that really what good vocabulary instruction looks like anyway? I sure didn't think so.

We needed to stop looking at vocabulary and content as two separate things. We needed a better way to introduce and reinforce new vocabulary without interrupting our instructional groove. But how?

I finally discovered concept sorts, which eventually evolved into Vocabulary Connection Cards. I don't remember where I first came in contact with concept sorts, but I loved them from the start. At first I didn't even recognize them as a vocabulary strategy, but the more I used them, the more I realized . . . this is it! This is how I could introduce and purposefully teach my students unfamiliar words while still focusing on the content as a whole. I didn't have to give vocabulary quizzes and grade lists of definitions copied from glossaries. My students' understanding of the new terms would be evident in their discussions, and eventually in their essays, which are a much better way to assess the true mastery of content I was aiming for.

They Are for Middle-School Teachers

Vocabulary Connection Cards would certainly work at a lower elementary level, and they would even work in high school! However, my own personal experiences are all in middle school, and I've found that this magical time when acne attacks, romance blossoms (and dies three weeks later), and social media comes "before anything else" is also the time when we are expected to start teaching more content than ever before. In kindergarten through third grade, social studies consists of doing an art project on Veteran's Day or holding a mock election to demonstrate democracy. Science is all about getting children interested in how plants grow and what it means to "hypothesize." And that is completely appropriate! The lower elementary grades focus more on reading, writing, and basic math—as they should be. By necessity, social studies and science at that level are more about increasing interest and awareness than imparting facts and content knowledge. In other words, kids don't have to understand all the steps in photosynthesis to grow a sunflower in a paper cup!

Once students hit middle school, things start to get real. Those little brains are capable of understanding bigger ideas, and to get to those bigger ideas, they need lots of information and lots of new words. Yet my husband is right in saying that we truly don't have time to teach vocabulary independent of content. Even if we did, vocabulary without context isn't effective in these content areas. That's where Vocabulary Connection Cards come in!

They Are Research Based

The Words Their Way series, published by Pearson, first popularized the use of all types of word sorts, including concept sorts, for increasing student comprehension. While most of the series focuses on sorting words based on morphology at the elementary level, a more in-depth look at the benefits of concept sorting—sorting words based on their meanings to show how they are connected—is provided in *Vocabulary Their Way: Word Study with Middle and Secondary Students* (Templeton et al., 2015). You can also find dozens of blogs and other articles on the Internet from classroom teachers, researchers, and professors promoting concept sorts as a highly effective instructional strategy; they have been used effectively in classrooms for decades!

This isn't surprising since concept sorts incorporate three of the ten strategies highlighted in *Classroom Instruction That Works: Research-Based Strategies for Increasing Student Achievement* (Marzano, Pickering, & Pollock, 2001): identifying similarities and differences, nonlinguistic representations, and cooperative learning. When done effectively, concept sorts can also integrate visual, auditory, and kinesthetic elements that appeal to all learning styles and allow students of all levels and abilities to participate and succeed.

In addition, doing concept sorts pushes students to the top two categories of the Instructional Practices Inventory (IPI)—a system of analyzing student engagement—developed by Jerry Valentine and Bryan Painter in 1996. Reasoning that the more engaged students are, the better their learning would be, Valentine and Painter developed a system that uses brief "snapshot"-style observations to determine the level of student engagement in a classroom. Years ago, every teacher in my school was trained to complete these observations and "code" student learning into one of the six categories listed in the chart on page 12.

As with any new observation system, I was leery at first. But I quickly realized that the IPI actually took the emphasis off me and put the focus on students. What I do doesn't matter as much, as long as it encourages students to actively engage with the content. For once, I wasn't the star of the show when an administrator walked in—students were! And that, in my opinion, is exactly as it should be. Furthermore, the IPI validated what I had already witnessed—students learn best when they are interacting with the content in a genuine, authentic way . . . and concept sorts are an excellent way to make that happen.

Instructional Practices Inventory Categories

BROAD CATEGORIES	CODING CATEGORIES	COMMON OBSERVER "LOOK-FORS"
Student-Engaged Instruction	Student Active Engaged Learning	Students are engaged in higher-order learning. Common examples include authentic project work, cooperative learning, hands-on learning, problem-based learning, demonstrations, and research.
	Student Learning Conversations	Students are engaged in active conversations that construct knowledge. Conversations may have been teacher stimulated but are not teacher dominated. Higher-order thinking is evident.
Teacher-Directed Instruction	Teacher-Led Instruction	Students are attentive to teacher-led learning experiences such as lecture, question and answer, teacher giving directions, and video instruction with teacher interaction. Discussion may occur, but instruction and ideas come primarily from the teacher.
	Student Work With Teacher Engaged	Students are doing seatwork, working on worksheets, book work, tests, video with teacher viewing the video with the students, etc. Teacher assistance or support is evident.
Disengagement	Student Work With Teacher Not Engaged	Students are doing seatwork, working on worksheets, book work, tests, video without teacher support, etc. Teacher assistance or support is not evident.
	Complete Disengagement	Students are not engaged in learning directly related to the curriculum.

(Valentine, 2005)

They Are Common Core Compatible

Regardless of what state you teach in or what set of standards you reference most, I'm confident that any standards worth their salt focus heavily on the importance of teaching students to define and use content-specific vocabulary. After all, "vocabulary knowledge is content knowledge" (Templeton et al., 2015, p. 3). The Common Core State Standards for Social Studies and Science are no exception.

Without true ownership of this type of vocabulary, students can't move on to the analysis and evaluation Benjamin Bloom and his colleagues told us to strive for back in 1956. Students can't form and defend their own opinions or explain their thinking to someone during a discussion. They can't even draw correct and educated conclusions

while reading the "news" on Facebook! (I know
. . . that's another educational topic altogether.)

By giving them ownership of essential
vocabulary, we can help students write and
reason about a topic more proficiently and
deeply. Vocabulary Connection Cards not
only build students' vocabulary, they also
provide ample opportunities to promote critical
thinking and writing skills.

In math, strategies like Connection Cards
are even more valuable given current standards'
increasing emphasis on mathematical reasoning
and student ownership of the process over
memorization of methods and equations. When
I was in school, if I could memorize a formula, I
could pass a test or quiz. I may not have any idea
why I was doing what I was doing and still get
100%. Today, that isn't the case . . . and rightly
so! We want students to know the why and how
behind those numbers and symbols and to be
able to change course if they get stuck—not stare
blankly and say, "But I memorized the formula!"

To that end, we want our students to be
able to talk about math. John Hattie, in *Visible
Learning for Teachers: Maximizing Impact on
Learning* (2012), points out that "the process of
talking math is essential for students learning
math. When they are comfortable producing the
language of math, then they have gained traction
with the concepts behind that language" (p. 194).
This is not something students are used to doing.
AT. ALL. In the past, math has been taught in
a very black and white, cut and dried, right or
wrong context. And indeed, there is very little
room for discussion about whether specific math
problems are right or wrong. But what students
can and should discuss in math is *why* they need
to know how to solve certain problems as well as
the context in which they might see those types
of problems in real life.

As the Common Core State Standards for
Mathematics points out, "Mathematics is not a list
of disconnected topics, tricks, or mnemonics;

The Common Core State Standards for Literacy in History/Social Studies, Science, and Technical Subjects

Social Studies
CCSS.ELA-LITERACY.RH.6-8.4
Determine the meaning of words
and phrases as they are used
in a text, including vocabulary
specific to domains related to
history/social studies.

Science
CCSS.ELA-LITERACY.RST.6-8.4
Determine the meaning of
symbols, key terms, and other
domain-specific words and
phrases as they are used in a
specific scientific or technical
context relevant to grades 6–8
texts and topics.

The Common Core State Standards for Mathematics

CCSS.MATH.PRACTICE.MP1
Make sense of problems and
persevere in solving them.

CCSS.MATH.PRACTICE.MP3
Construct viable arguments and
critique the reasoning of others.

it is a coherent body of knowledge made up of interconnected concepts." Vocabulary Connection Cards could not be more perfectly suited to this new approach to math, requiring the traditional understanding of those mathematical terms and formulas, but also pushing students to discuss and explain why those formulas work.

They Show Students the Bigger Picture

The bottom line is, teaching new words is just as important outside of ELA as it is inside the language arts classroom—maybe more so! And yet the traditional methods of teaching vocabulary often seem almost counterproductive to our goals: They take too much of our valuable time without providing a deep-enough understanding of critical key terms. The solution is to present new vocabulary words not as individual items to be graded on the next quiz, but as puzzle pieces that, once mastered, can be put together to create a bigger picture. Memorize a definition without true understanding, and all you have when you're finished is a single puzzle piece. But figure out how all those pieces fit together, and in the end you've got a masterpiece you can slather in Mod Podge and hang on your wall! And that's TRUE content mastery!

Chapter Two

Vocabulary Connection Cards in Action

If you haven't heard of concept sorts, get ready to change the way you think about great lesson planning. Think the best lessons have to take hours to plan and be packed with bells and whistles? Wrong! It doesn't get much simpler—or much more effective—than a concept sort. Not only do concept sorts deepen students' knowledge of content, they are also EXTREMELY LOW PREP! That's right . . . this strategy will increase student learning and SAVE YOU TIME. You can't afford NOT to try it! If I sound like an infomercial—well, don't send your three easy payments of $29.99 to me. Concept sorts have been around for a long time. This strategy is an oldie, but goodie! Here's the gist:

How to Conduct a Basic Concept Sort

1 **Choose 25 to 35 words that are associated with your unit of study.** We'll be calling these Vocabulary Connection Cards. You can have more or less, but I've found that 25 to 35 words work best for my 7th graders. The number of words is not as important as *which* words you choose!

A typical concept sort features only the vocabulary that is essential to the unit of study. I've found, however, that my students make deeper connections when the sort consists of some new vocabulary along with "supporting words" they should already know. To that end, I create Vocabulary Connection Cards by including each of the following three types of words:

- **New, essential words**—words students don't know yet (for example, *communism, denominator, photosynthesis*)
- **Known content words**—words students already know that are specific to the unit (for example, *China, equals, light*)
- **Supporting words**—words that could be used to view the unit subjectively or that prompt deeper thinking about the unit (for example, *fair, different, cause, effect*)

That last category of words is what makes this strategy very effective! Students often don't immediately see how these words connect to other vocabulary in the unit and are challenged to think outside the box and stretch to make those deeper connections.

To come up with some good supporting words, ask yourself these questions:

- Is there anything in this unit about which students could have a debate or argument? What words might they use to defend their opinion?

- Does this unit require students to think about or make choices? What words could be used to describe or evaluate their options?

- What are the real-world applications for this unit? Are there any words you could include that would lead students to make that connection?

- Are there any analogies students could draw between this unit and another unrelated topic? What words might help them see the similarities?

- Is there a critical structure, or way of organizing the information, in the unit that students should recognize (for example, cause and effect, compare and contrast, chronological order)? What words will they need to illustrate that structure?

Don't stress out too much about choosing all the perfect words or about which category the words go in. Your students will surprise you by making connections you didn't even consider, using whatever words you give them. And you can always add or remove words as the day goes on. Like many lessons, Vocabulary Connection Cards will improve as you use them over time.

Here is a sample list for a unit on the American Revolution:

NEW WORDS	KNOWN WORDS	SUPPORTING WORDS
MILITIA	GREAT BRITAIN	FAIR
CONTINENTAL ARMY	COLONIES	AGREE
REVOLUTION	KING	WIN
CONSTITUTION	FRANCE	LOSE
DEMOCRACY	TAXES	RISK
MONARCHY	LOYAL	POWER
STAMP ACT	LIBERTY	
BOSTON TEA PARTY	WASHINGTON	
RED COATS	GOVERNMENT	
PATRIOTS		
CORNWALLIS		
JEFFERSON		
TREATY OF PARIS		
LEXINGTON & CONCORD		
DECLARATION OF INDEPENDENCE		

For certain content, you may find it helpful to go beyond words and add a few pictures. As Robert Marzano, Debra Pickering, and Jane Pollock point out in *Classroom Instruction That Works: Research-Based Strategies for Increasing Student Achievement* (2001), "One of the best ways to learn a new word is to associate an image with it" (p. 126). In addition, sometimes certain concepts can be taken to a deeper level using pictures. Don't go crazy—six or seven pictures is plenty. Adding too many can shift the focus away from the vocabulary you are trying to highlight. And make sure you choose pictures with a purpose. Pictures should illustrate a particularly abstract concept or promote connections with real life or other content areas. For example, the pictures below could be added to the American Revolution concept sort to help students make visual connections between words such as *monarchy* and *democracy*.

Monarchy

Democracy

2 **Write or type each word on a separate slip of paper, note card, or sticky note.** My goal as a teacher is to make things as easy on myself as possible while still getting awesome results for my kiddos. When I create a set of Vocabulary Connection Cards, I simply open a blank document on my computer, set my font size to about 48 points, and start typing. I double or triple space the words to make sure there's room to cut them apart, and then I print however many sets I need. I use the paper cutter to slice them up, and *voilà!* they're ready to go. If you want to reinforce the actual spelling of the words with your students, you might consider having them write their own sets on 3-by-5 note cards or sticky notes. Or if you want to go somewhere in the middle, print out the sets, but have students cut them apart for you. I am all for putting students to work, so no judgments here! ("Hey guys, you know what would be super fun??? Scraping gum off the bottoms of your desks! Let's see who can collect the most wads before recess!")

3 **Divide the class into small groups.** The magic number in my experience is three or four students per group. Discussions among students are what make this strategy work, so you want to make sure the groups are small enough for everyone to be heard, but not so small that conversation stalls. You also want to try to group students based on who will work comfortably together. I've found this depends less on student ability level and more on social personality. A group of students who all struggle academically *can* do this activity and benefit from it just as well as a heterogeneous group containing some high and some low kids—as long as they are willing to talk to one another!

For this reason, you may find that Vocabulary Connection Cards is an activity that improves as the year goes on. The more comfortable students become with one another, the better their conversations will be. The group that sits in awkward silence during Unit 1 may conduct a college-level debate in Unit 8. That being said, it is also a good idea to switch up groups from time to time. This exposes students to more viewpoints and challenges them to work with a variety of personalities.

4 **Give each group a large, flat space to work on and one set of Vocabulary Connection Cards.** Instruct students to organize the words however they think is best. If you want to see them really sweat, refuse to give them any further guidance! This can be really fun, but you will inevitably have someone who convinces his or her group to put the words in alphabetical order . . . because, middle school. If you want to avoid this, I recommend saying something like this:

"I'm giving you a set of words. All of these words have SOMETHING to do with the unit we've been studying. Your group's job is to organize them. You can group them, categorize them, create a graphic organizer out of them . . . whatever you want as long as your decisions are based on what you know—or think you know—about the meaning of those words. There are MANY right ways to do this, so don't worry about getting it 'right.' Focus on being able to explain your thinking. Ready . . . set . . . go!"

Presenting the activity this way with little guidance is called an "open sort" (Templeton et al., 2015, p. 38). This is my favorite way to use Vocabulary Connection Cards because it truly challenges students and requires them to use their brains to "see" the relationships between the words. It also allows for them to go beyond simply placing the words into categories and opens the door to word webs, graphic organizers, and more. However, if your students need more support, an excellent differentiation strategy would be to provide headings for some basic categories you would like them to sort the words into. This is called a "closed sort" (Templeton et al., 2015, p. 38).

5 **Give students enough time to sort the cards, while you walk around and LISTEN as they work.** You will be amazed at the depth of some of the conversations you will hear—and that is really the beauty of Vocabulary Connection Cards! But notice I said, *LISTEN.* Do not help them! Respond to any questions they may have with, "What does your group think about that?" Say it enough times, and they'll get the idea. Resist the urge to correct them when you

Students discussing where each card should go and why

overhear an incorrect statement: "Wasn't Cornwallis the King of Great Britain?" Because nine times out of ten, your students will impress you by correcting one another. "No . . . remember he was fighting Washington? I think he was a general or something . . ." And the few times they don't correct each other will turn out to be great learning opportunities too!

If you choose, you may allow students to use their notes. I figure if they are organized and motivated enough to look up something in their notes or textbook, that's a skill I'd like their group mates to learn too!

6 **Help students finish up.** You will always have one group that finishes far ahead of the others. I like to walk by and give their words a very critical stare before silently walking away, shaking my head. That usually gets them back to work and prompts some entertaining and slightly panicked whispers and arguments.

Inevitably there will be one or two groups who are left staring at a handful of words that none of them are able or willing to categorize. If enough time has passed for them to have really struggled with this, and you can tell they aren't making any progress, have them place those words upside down off to the side of their work area. This instruction will be met with sighs of relief!

But don't YOU forget about those set-aside words! Those lonely, forgotten cards are juicy little morsels of data just waiting for you to put to good use! Once, while doing a sort, I noticed that all seven groups in my class had been unable to categorize the same word. Using this formative assessment data *(Can I get an administrator in here to observe this?!)*, I was able to design the next day's bell work to revisit that trouble spot. And I didn't even have to grade any formal assessment to do it!

7 **Share and discuss students' completed sorts.** Below is an example of how a group completed their sort for the American Revolution unit mentioned earlier.

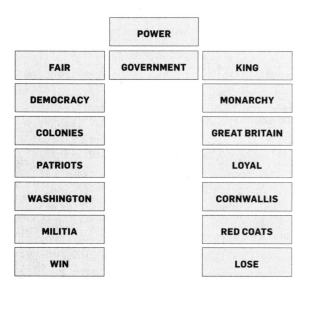

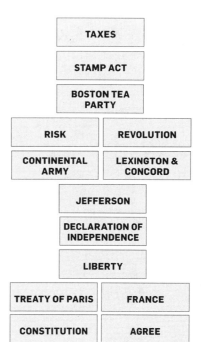

In this sort, students clearly understood the contrasts between the two forms of government engaged in the Revolutionary War (see left side of sort). By placing the word *power* at the top of those groups, students indicated their understanding that *government* is about the distribution of power—a critical concept in this unit. On the right side, students arranged the remaining words in a timeline or chain of events. Taxes, such as the Stamp Act, led to protests like the Boston Tea Party. When that didn't work, colonists risked revolution, and the Continental Army fought battles like those at Lexington and Concord. Thomas Jefferson wrote the Declaration of Independence to proclaim liberty from Great Britain, and eventually, with the help of France, we signed the Treaty of Paris, ending the war. Then the colonies began the arduous process of agreeing on a Constitution.

Of course, just by completing the sort, students have engaged with the vocabulary at a high level and have had to synthesize their knowledge with the opinions of their classmates. However, the process of explaining their sorts can be just as valuable. "Dialogue is seen as an essential tool for learning, . . . and teachers can learn so much about their effect on student learning by listening to students thinking aloud" (Hattie, 2012, p. 74). This can be done with peers or through teacher-led discussions. Take this small section from the sort on page 19.

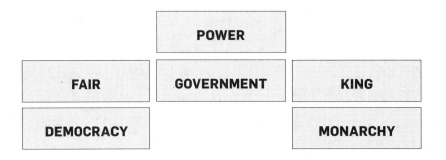

Just to explain this part of the sort, students would have to verbalize in their own words the basic differences between *democracy* and *monarchy* and explain why both belong under the heading of *power*. In addition, they would have to defend their assertion that democracy is *fair*—which will require even deeper interaction with the content, demonstrating just how valuable those "supporting words" can be! Stay tuned for more information on student discussions later.

Another group of students sorted the same set of words a different way (see page 21). While the left section of this sort is similar to the first version in that it follows a timeline of events, there are some noticeable differences. Since the sort included the word *fair*, but not *unfair*, this group thought creatively and placed the word *fair* upside down to indicate that taxes, such as the Stamp Act, were examples of unfair treatment by the British monarchy. (This is exactly the kind of creativity I LOVE to see!) In addition, the transition from monarchy to a constitutional democracy is imbedded in the chain of events, essentially bookending the timeline. The smaller group of cards on the right is arranged almost as a scoreboard of the war itself, noting key players, leaders, and results, as well as key battles.

I always encourage my students to be creative and purposeful in their arrangements of the words on the table. For some reason, they usually think at first that they must keep

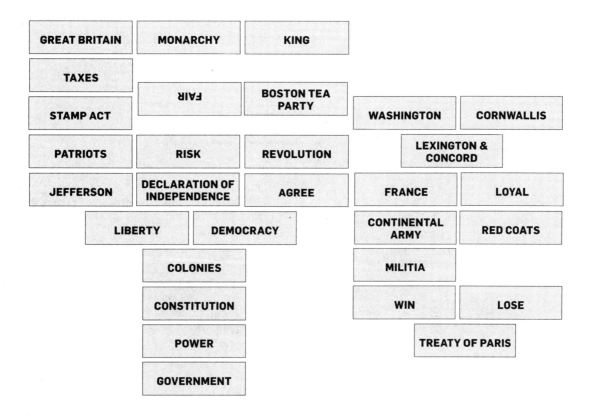

the words in nice neat rows or columns. But often that is not how the brain, or the content itself, works! Real concepts can be messy and complex and overlapping in nature, and I want students' finished sorts to reflect that.

Most of all, it is very important to stress to students that there is an unlimited number of "right" ways to sort. I'm certain my students are tired of hearing me say, "It's not about getting it right, it's about explaining what you know!" According to Hattie (2012), there are six "signposts" of great teaching. Number 5 reads:

> *Teachers need to move from the single idea to multiple ideas, and to relate*
> *and then extend these ideas such that learners construct, and reconstruct,*
> *knowledge and ideas. It is not the knowledge or ideas, but the learner's*
> *construction of these knowledge and ideas that is critical* (p. 19).

Vocabulary Connection Cards are the epitome of this signpost because they illustrate to many students for the first time that these words are not just terms to memorize for the test and that learning is about understanding and vocalizing complex concepts in their own way, on their own terms. In addition, seeing the varied ways their classmates have sorted the same words can often open students' eyes to a new way of approaching the content, which can lead to the "aha!" moment we teachers are always trying create.

Including pictures in a sort can make the connections even richer and more varied! For example, in the following sort about percentages, students in one group used the word *choice* to indicate that there are two different ways to solve the problem 15% of 57.

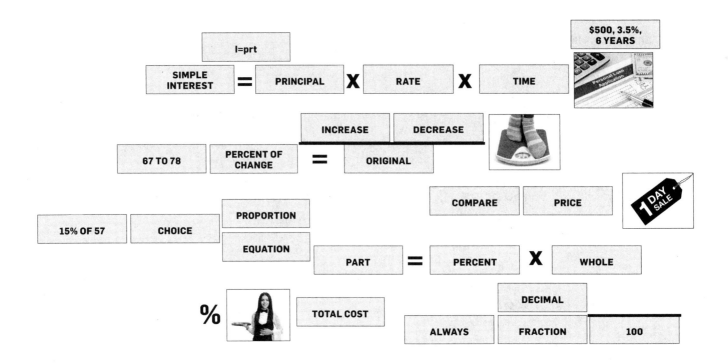

But check out how another group used the word *choice*:

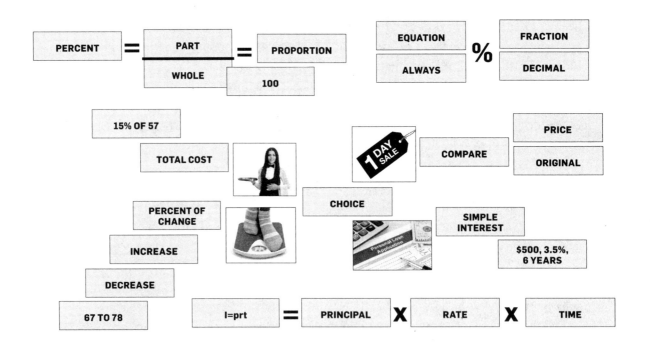

During our whole-class discussion, this group pointed out that in every real-life scenario presented in the pictures, we are making a choice. The students explained that we often choose what we purchase at a restaurant or store based on what the total cost (with tax or tip) will be, that we choose to purchase something when it goes on sale for a certain percentage off the original price, and that we choose whether to get a loan based on the interest rate. They even pointed out that we can choose to eat or exercise more to impact our percent of weight gain or loss! This sort may not be as clear when it comes to the formulas and equations themselves, but the students have a firm grasp of how and when these math concepts could impact them in real life . . . and isn't that really the goal?

From here, there are a number of ways you can go. But even if students packed it up right here and called it a day, they have had learning conversations that would otherwise have been absent. Score!

A Word About Student Conversation Skills

Crappy.

Okay, maybe I'm being a little bit harsh. Honestly, most of the time I feel that kids at this age group thrive when you allow them to talk to one another. I rarely have students who don't want to participate, and when I do, some gentle prodding from me and/or careful placement in a group of students with whom they feel comfortable can usually overcome that reluctance. But sometimes, even when I have carefully chosen my groups and things should be going well, their conversations could go something along these lines:

Overachieving Oliver: This goes here! And this goes here . . . and we could put this here! (*Starts shuffling cards quicker than a casino dealer and creates a beautiful word web*)

Agreeable Amy: Yeah, that makes sense. (*Nodding enthusiastically as she pushes more cards toward Oliver*)

Shy Sharon: Okaaaay . . . (*Trying to hide behind her hair*)

To avoid this problem, it may be helpful to conduct a mini-lesson on how to have a good learning conversation. In a wonderful article on *Edutopia*, Dr. Allen Mendler (2013) points out that "learning to listen and talk is an extremely important way to broaden knowledge, enhance understanding, and build community." He offers some great tips and helpful strategies for how to help students (or your own children) learn this invaluable life skill—such as, passing an object around the group to encourage turn-taking, and helping students recognize nonverbal cues, such as nodding and eye contact.

If you are feeling theatrical, you might consider getting a few of your colleagues to

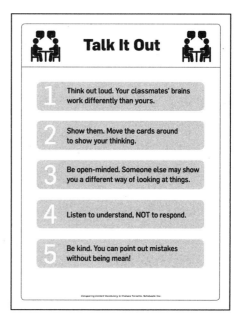

Talk It Out

1. Think out loud. Your classmates' brains work differently than yours.

2. Show them. Move the cards around to show your thinking.

3. Be open-minded. Someone else may show you a different way of looking at things.

4. Listen to understand, NOT to respond.

5. Be kind. You can point out mistakes without being mean!

Conquering Content Vocabulary © Chelsea Tornetto, Scholastic Inc.

Strategies for positive learning conversations

help you act out a scene similar to the one described above. Students LOVE seeing their teachers pretend to be students, and when they are in their groups later and someone isn't participating constructively, they can always say, "Don't be like Mr. Smith!" taking the blame off the student and deflecting it in a less-threatening direction.

If theater isn't your thing (it isn't mine), use the reproducible mini-poster on page 25 to review positive techniques for learning conversations with your students. Start with a topic they are familiar with and allow them to practice a bit. (Using this as a "getting to know you" activity at the start of the year is a great idea!) Completing this mini-lesson beforehand also gives you some handy-dandy catchphrases to guide student conversations later in the year: "Don't forget to think out loud!"

With all this being said, I have seen the power of Vocabulary Connection Cards to reach students who struggle in a typical learning environment. Just this past school year, one of my special-education students whose IEP states that he "refuses to speak in an academic setting," sat up in his chair, leaned forward, and quietly contributed to his group's discussion. On top of that, he actually understood more of the content than his group mates did and was able to guide and even correct them multiple times. He wouldn't participate in the whole-class discussion afterwards, but I could tell that in just those few minutes, his classmates saw him in a different light—and to be honest, so did I! Before, I hadn't been able to tell how much he was comprehending, but clearly he was catching more than I thought he had been! I began carefully calling on him when I knew he knew the answers and was able to coax him out of his shell gradually, even if just minimally. There were still days when he struggled to engage, but we made progress. And it all started with Vocabulary Connection Cards.

The following chapters illustrate how that original set of words can be used at any point during a unit of study. As you will see, you can conceivably utilize Connection Cards before, during, and after learning. However, we all know that overusing even the best strategy can easily kill the novelty of it, making it less effective for students and less fun for teachers. So don't feel like you need to use Connection Cards repeatedly throughout the unit to see results. Instead, choose the time when you think your students would benefit most, and go for it!

Chapter Wrap-Up

- Choose 25 to 35 words from any unit of study. Be sure to include new, known, and supporting words.

- Type or write the words on small cards or slips of paper.

- Divide the class into groups of three or four students. Form groups based on who will talk and work well together.

- Tell students to arrange the words based on what they've learned. There are many correct ways to sort!

- Listen and observe.

- Allow students to set aside unknown words. Collect that data!

- Share and discuss the completed sorts.

Talk It Out

1 Think out loud. Your classmates' brains work differently than yours.

2 Show them. Move the cards around to show your thinking.

3 Be open-minded. Someone else may show you a different way of looking at things.

4 Listen to understand, NOT to respond.

5 Be kind. You can point out mistakes without being mean!

Chapter Three

The Three Stages of Vocabulary Instruction

There are three stages to vocabulary instruction:

1. **Introducing students to unknown words**

2. **Explaining the definitions of those words**

3. **Providing students with multiple opportunities to use and master those words in conversation and in writing**

Most teachers, particularly outside of ELA, tend to focus on the second stage—informing students of the meanings of new words—while often completely neglecting the importance of Stages 1 and 3. (In fact, Marzano's "Six-Step Vocabulary Process" [2004] doesn't even mention the first stage. Hey, I should write a book about this stuff! Oh . . . wait . . .) Vocabulary Connection Cards help shift the focus to the first and third stages, exposing students to new words in a way that generates engagement, linking the new words to students' prior knowledge, providing the opportunity for deeper connections, and encouraging student ownership of each word as a part of their working vocabulary.

STAGE 1
Introducing Unknown Words

So let's rewind a bit. You've created your Vocabulary Connection Cards, but your unit of study hasn't started yet. You know you're going to do a concept sort once your students have been introduced to the new vocabulary, but how do you begin? The following activities show you how to use Vocabulary Connection Cards to introduce new words to students (without overwhelming or intimidating them) and how to gather pre-assessment data and activate students' prior knowledge.

Getting Students' Attention: Mystery Unit

Teachers will do just about anything to get students interested and engaged at the beginning of a new unit. You know what I mean—the history teacher who shows up dressed as George Washington at the beginning of the unit on the Revolutionary War, or the science teacher who rolls in on a skateboard to introduce the Laws of Motion. While these kinds of "dramatic entrances" will certainly get kids' attention (and might make you temporarily famous on YouTube), they seldom get students engaged in learning.

The challenge is to find something that not only captures students' interest but also gets their brains to dig into the actual learning that needs to take place. Since I am not the theatrical type anyway, I often try to get kids interested by encouraging them to do something that most kids are really, really good at—talking. And Vocabulary Connection Cards are a great way to get the conversation started.

Divide the class into small groups (I partner up students) and hand each group a set of Vocabulary Connection Cards for the upcoming unit. As described in Chapter 2, some of these words will be familiar to them and some definitely will not. Using only these "clues," challenge students to come up with the title and one or more learning objectives for the unit ahead. If writing an entire objective seems too challenging for students, consider posting the objective with the most important words missing and asking them to fill in the blanks. Once all the groups have finished, invite each one to share their answers with the class. Or simply reveal the real learning objectives for students to compare to their own.

There are several things I like about this. First, listening to the conversations among students during this activity tells me a lot about what background knowledge they have and where they are on their learning journey. Second, it gives me a chance to remind students what an "objective" really is. (Can you say, "summer break"?) Third, and probably most surprising, is how my often disinterested and easily distracted students suddenly develop an interest in these new words . . . WAY before I even give them any instructions!

The first time I tried this activity, I honestly felt a little demoralized. I mean, how many times had I started an activity by passing out what I thought was a very high-interest article or reading piece—with pictures and diagrams and tons of "cool" stuff—and had students roll their eyes with exhaustion and look away? And here, all I did was give them a few words on slips of paper, and before I could even explain the goal of the activity, the questions were coming at me fast and furious: "What are these for?" "Why did you spell *summer* S-U-M-E-R?" "What does *surplus* mean?" "Ooooh! I already know what *cause* and *effect* mean!" "I bet this is about Ancient Egypt." "Can I go to the bathroom?" Okay . . . so that last one is just to make you feel like you are in a real classroom, but you get the idea.

Using Vocabulary Connection Cards as clues, two students try to guess the new unit of study.

Pretty quickly I realized, students are used to reading articles. They are used to lists of words and definitions. Nowadays they are even used to highly engaging activities that get them out of their seats, find partners, or act things out. But this stack of seemingly random words just dropped on the desk in front of them was novel and weird . . . and, best of all, mysterious.

When the brain reads an article, it doesn't have to figure out much. If the article is well-written and at the appropriate grade level, all students have to do is read it and be mentally present while they do. Easy! But with Vocabulary Connection Cards, the purpose of the new words isn't spelled out for them, so their brain automatically starts trying to make meaning of it. All the tricks I usually use to get kids to engage with new information—think-pair-share, annotating text, written responses—weren't necessary because they were engaging on their own. The activity is more interesting for students AND requires them to think deeper.

Presenting the objectives as a "mystery" and giving students the opportunity to "win" by solving it engender interest, while the "clues" on the cards engage students by forcing them to activate their prior knowledge of the vocabulary. It may not get as many YouTube views as that chemistry teacher who set a hundred-dollar bill on fire, but it gets kids actually thinking about important content. And besides, you really shouldn't start setting things on fire until at least third quarter, right?

Tracking the Data: Pre-Assessment Sort

A quick look at the education boards on Pinterest will tell you that tracking each student's learning is all the rage—and with good reason. Gathering the right information about your students' learning during a unit can make the assessment at the end feel like you just reached the summit of a particularly tough mountain, instead of getting pushed down one. As formative assessment experts Larry Ainsworth and Donald Viegut (2006) explain, "Teachers become confident that their students will succeed on the common summative assessment because they wisely used the results of their common formative assessments to make needed 'mid-course' corrections ahead of time" (p. 37). If gathering this formative assessment data is on your to-do list, Vocabulary Connection Cards can be a great place to start. By focusing students' attention on key vocabulary associated with the unit, you give them (and yourself) a concrete and simple way to measure progress, while still allowing yourself the flexibility to collect data on those words in a variety of ways.

To get started, give each student his or her own set of Vocabulary Connection Cards. Instruct students to sort the cards into three categories: words they know the meaning of, words they are unsure about, and words they definitely don't know. Feel free to be creative in naming those categories. In the past, I have used green, yellow, and red to mimic

All images created at www.bitmoji.com.

traffic lights (see page 32). You can even use emojis! If you want to have some real fun, use Bitmoji.com to create some that look just like you. Kids love it!

To save time, you could eliminate some of those "supporting words" (e.g., *fair, similar*) we talked about in Chapter 2 at this stage. But sometimes I find that leaving them in actually helps me identify which kids are really struggling. For example, a 7th grader who is unable to write a definition for the word *similar* might be one I need to keep my eye on!

Next, you may choose to allow students to share and discuss their results with a partner or group. I find that although NOT allowing discussion gives me a more accurate picture of what students know, allowing them to help one another often builds up some much-needed confidence. Providing time for discussion also introduces just enough peer pressure to prevent that one lazy kiddo from putting every single word in the "Don't Know It" category just to drive you crazy!

After students have sorted their cards, there are a few ways you could go to get that all-important formative assessment data:

1 **If you like to track the data yourself,** have students write definitions of only the words they have placed in the "Know It" category on the back of each card, on a sheet of paper, or on a chart like the one below, and turn it in to you as a ticket-out-the-door.

This will give you a more accurate view of which words they really do know and which ones they only think they know. After you have checked them, you will have a number correct out of the total number of essential terms, which you can then record wherever you record your data. The best part about this is you only have to decipher their lovely handwriting for the definitions they felt confident about, instead of reading 15 to 20 painfully incorrect definitions from each student!

To continue tracking students' growth, simply return their charts to them at various points throughout the unit and allow them to revise and add to their definitions. Each time you collect and check their charts, you will have a new snapshot of how your students are doing.

Name: _____	Date: _____
Ancient Civilizations Vocabulary	

Write a definition for each term you KNOW below. Skip the ones you don't know!

complex institutions	cities
specialized workers	record keeping
improved technology	civilization
Sumer	scribes
metalworking	Catal Huyuk
surplus	hunter-gatherer
irrigation	cuneiform

Have students write the definitions of only the words they actually know.

2 **If you prefer for students to track their own data,** give each student three labeled envelopes to keep in his or her binder or folder. As the unit progresses, have students revisit their envelopes to see if they are able to move any words from the "Maybe" and "Don't Know It" categories to the "Know It" group. Or, if the thought of 30 students each keeping track of three envelopes with 25 to 35 slips of paper inside makes you twitch, just give them a chart (like the one shown on page 32) and allow them to track their own progress.

In *Visible Learning for Teachers* (2012), Hattie lists goal setting and self-monitoring as "among the most effective strategies" for improving student achievement, and I couldn't agree more. There is real power in making students active participants in the process of recording and tracking their goals and achievements. It takes away the dynamic of the teacher "giving" students grades and puts the emphasis on students earning them. And when you see a student looking confidently at a fat envelope full of the new words he or she has learned, you'll know what I mean!

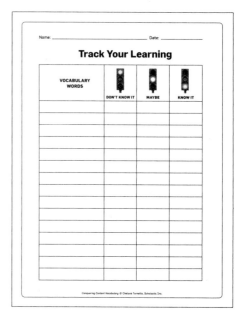

Distribute copies of this chart to students so they can track their own progress in learning content vocabulary.

3 **If you prefer to track whole-class data,** do a quick tally of the results of students' individual sorts. Ask, for example, *"How many of you put capitalism in the 'Don't Know It' category?"* To avoid students changing their answer due to peer pressure or embarrassment, you might have them cover their eyes while you do this. Post a large version of the "Track Your Learning" chart along with a class set of Vocabulary Connection Cards on a prominent bulletin board or wall to show where the majority of students placed each word. Throughout the unit, refer back to the words and do another quick tally to see if any words have moved into the "Know It" category. This strategy is particularly effective because it provides you with data and serves as a visual reminder to students of what the unit is all about.

Enlisting Students' Help

Once students have gotten the idea about Vocabulary Connection Cards, you may choose to step things up a notch! This activity depends on the personalities and reading abilities of students in your classroom. Note: You may want to avoid this activity if you have a lot of struggling readers or students who get easily frustrated. However, if you're trying to differentiate for some careful readers who enjoy a challenge, this would be perfect for them!

Rather than presenting students with the Vocabulary Connection Cards right off the bat, give them a reading piece that is central to your unit, such as a section from the textbook. Tell them that this reading piece will be the focus of the upcoming unit and ask them to identify 10 to 15 key vocabulary words that will be important for the class to know. Give students plenty of time to read and choose their words carefully.

This challenges higher-level students to read something unfamiliar—requiring them to use context clues and so on—but still gives them an "out." After all, they don't really have to know what each unfamiliar word means; they merely have to determine if it seems important to understanding the text. You can then include some or all of the words they selected in the Vocabulary Connection Cards for that unit. They will feel super smart having helped "choose" what they will be learning next!

Stage 1 Wrap-Up

Stage 1 is all about highlighting key vocabulary words that students will need to "own" in order to understand the unit. By exposing students to these unfamiliar words up front, you take some of the fear out of future encounters and help them know where to focus their attention in upcoming reading passages.

- Vocabulary Connection Cards, which at first may appear to be a random collection of words, naturally engage students in activating prior knowledge and making meaning.

- Pre-assessment sorts are a simple way to gather data. Resorting throughout the unit allows easy tracking of student progress.

- Challenge advanced learners to create Vocabulary Connection Cards for the next unit.

Name: _____ Date: _____

Track Your Learning

VOCABULARY WORDS	DON'T KNOW IT	MAYBE	KNOW IT

Explaining the Meaning of Unknown Words

Once you've introduced the words to the class, it's time for the second stage of vocabulary instruction—explaining the meaning of new words. Vocabulary Connection Cards, as I mentioned earlier, focus on Stages 1 and 3, so this stage is about you finding the best way to explain the meaning of new words to your students. It may depend on a number of things— the type of content, your students' age, their learning styles . . . even the time of day or year can make a difference in how you choose to provide instruction. (Have you ever tried teaching new vocabulary to middle schoolers the day after Halloween? Yeah, me neither.) The important thing is that you find ways to encourage students to make CONNECTIONS between those words. Below are a few of my favorite strategies, but do what works best for you.

Designing Reading Guides

Rather than giving students a list of words and definitions to copy into their notes, I design my note-taking lesson to help them make natural connections between new words and their prior knowledge. I got this idea from my husband, Mike, who adapted it from the Textbook Activity Guides described in *Reading History: A Practical Guide to Improving Literacy* by Janet Allen (2005).

To design a reading guide, think about how you would like your students to think and what connections you want them to make as they are reading a new text, and then formulate questions to lead them down that path. The reading guide is intended to model good thinking, so as the year progresses students begin to naturally look for those connections on their own. It's more of an art than a science.

When guiding them through a section about Siberia, for example, the reading guide might look like the one at right. This type of questioning leads students through new vocabulary independently and prompts them to draw from their personal prior knowledge,

Name: _____   Date: _____

What are some situations where you might hear or use the word *permanent*?
_____
_____

Explain in your own words what the word *permanent* means.
_____
_____

Now, read "A Challenging Climate" on page 50. Based on what you know about the word *permanent* and the new information you read in the text, what do you think *permafrost* is?
_____
_____

In the space below, draw a picture or diagram that will help you remember that definition.

Sample reading guide for a unit on Siberia

which is the key to true comprehension. By starting with something familiar then helping them make the logical connection to a new, unfamiliar word, you not only make it more likely that students will retain that knowledge, you also make tackling a new word seem less intimidating.

Usually I have my students complete these reading guides with a partner first, then go over them together as a class to allow for sharing and discussion. When doing partner work, I find it helpful to limit students' resources to make them more dependent on discussion and working together. For example, I might give Student 1 the textbook and Student 2 the reading guide. Student 1 reads a section of the text aloud while Student 2 listens carefully for the answers to the questions on the reading guide. Then they discuss and agree on an answer, and Student 2 records it. Every few questions they switch roles. This serves two purposes:

- First, it forces students to really interact with the text and with each other. It's very difficult to fly through, writing down surface-level, thoughtless answers when you can't refer back to the text yourself. Student 2 is dependent on Student 1 to reread any difficult passages, and Student 1 is dependent on Student 2 to clearly explain the questions and guide them to the next reading passage.

- Second, since a good reading guide asks students to connect new words to prior knowledge, two heads are always better than one. In the example on page 33, one student alone may not be able to think of a situation in which the word *permanent* might be used, but a partner is likely to be able to help come up with something. A bit of back-and-forth conversation is essential in forming strong mental connections.

Every reading guide is a mental path I create to show students how good readers think as they read. Reading, after all, is the most common and natural way we add new words to our working vocabulary. When was the last time *you* sat down with a dictionary and a list of new words? And yet, I'm sure you've learned a new word or two since you graduated from school, most likely through reading!

Having a whole-class discussion of the completed reading guides and sharing students' explanations and drawings solidify their understanding even further. As a bonus, students can use the completed reading guides as additional study guides for the formal assessment.

Connecting With Pictures

Another way to help students absorb new meanings is to associate each new word and definition with an image. For example, in the first unit of my 6th-grade world history course, I introduce the five traits of civilization: *cities, specialized workforce, improved technology, complex institutions*, and *record keeping*. To communicate the definitions of these terms to my students, we read aloud a section from the textbook and come up with student-friendly definitions together. I hate textbook glossaries. Even if the vocabulary used wasn't way over my students' heads, the overly formal tone and structure is often enough to keep kids confused. For example, compare the following two definitions of *karma*:

TEXTBOOK GLOSSARY	STUDENT FRIENDLY
karma—in Hinduism, the consequences of a person's actions in this life, which determine his or her fate in the next life*	**karma**—the Hindu belief that your actions in this life decide what happens to you in the next life

* from World Cultures and Geography *(McDougal Littell, 2008)*

Simply removing the words *consequences*, *determine*, and *fate* has probably made this definition accessible to twice as many students. I am all about challenging students' reading levels, but not while they are learning new content vocabulary! Make sure all the words within your definitions are words your students feel comfortable using in their day-to-day conversations.

After writing down those student-friendly definitions, I show the class a series of pictures that represent one or more of the new terms. With a partner, students discuss which trait of civilization each picture best represents. Then we discuss their answers as a class. I carefully choose some pictures that clearly illustrate one trait or another and some that students could argue represent multiple traits. This forces them to a deeper level of thinking and requires them to really analyze the meaning of the terms. For example, I might use this photo, top right, to represent "record keeping." This photo is fairly straightforward. It clearly shows an example of cuneiform, which was one of the earliest forms of record keeping.

A cuneiform

However, to prompt some deeper thinking, I might present students with this photo, bottom right. This photo is definitely an example of "improved technology"—the modern sewing machine is a huge advancement over sewing by hand. But because the workers shown in the picture are experts at operating these machines, providing clothing and other textiles for the entire

Textile workers sewing clothes

community, the picture is also an excellent example of a "specialized workforce."

Another example is this photo of Washington, D.C., at right. Students might argue that because it shows the Capitol Building, the photo best represents "complex institutions" (the term for government, religions, and other organizations that give structure to society.) But it also clearly depicts a "city," and the traffic lights, lampposts, and cars are excellent examples of "improved technology." Of course, in order to have these types of discussions, students must have

The Capitol Building in Washington, D.C.

a real grasp of the meanings of all five traits of civilization—which is precisely the point! Making connections requires and builds comprehension.

Definition Discovery

One of the best ways to force students to make connections with new words is to require them to use context clues. If you simply give them a reading passage that contains unfamiliar terms, they may do this, but typically each word is used only once or twice and in such similar context that it isn't very helpful to students. For example, your math textbook will only refer to the word *fraction* in terms of . . . well, fractions! Instead, provide students with three or four sentences that use the same unfamiliar term (or a slightly different form of it) in a variety of ways and have students use those context clues to determine the meaning of the word. With *fractions*, for example, I might present students with these sentences:

> *The winning runner crossed the finish line a **fraction** of a second before her opponent.*

> *The mirror fell from the wall and **fractured** into a thousand pieces.*

> *My mom makes me put a small **fraction** of my birthday money in the bank each year.*

Using these sentences, which would hopefully be somewhat familiar to students, they should be able to deduce the meaning of the word *fraction*. I can then give them a student-friendly definition to write in their notes, but using their own prior knowledge to arrive at that definition will make it much more likely they will remember it.

Of course, this strategy can't be used with some uber content-specific terms. (Have you ever tried using *Joseph Stalin* in three different contexts?) But when it works, it's well worth the time.

Stage 2 Wrap-Up

Whatever strategy you use, I recommend these three things that will make utilizing Vocabulary Connection Cards easier as you proceed with the unit.

- Always encourage and emphasize mental connections between the new words and students' prior knowledge. "When we read something new, we are much more likely to understand it if we see connections that make it relevant" (Gallagher, 2004, p. 27). Prior knowledge is essential. It may feel like you are getting off topic or wasting class time, but trust me, you aren't. If students don't have any of their own prior knowledge, give them some. Tell a funny story about the time you "fractured" your arm. Describe that tense moment when your golf ball stopped only a "fraction" of an inch from the hole. Or let them talk to one another! Taking time to activate their prior knowledge will pay dividends when you introduce them to a new word in an instructional setting.

- Make sure that at some point you require students to write down the meaning of each vocabulary word. This way, students have something to fall back on when they are at home or in study hall and can't remember what happened in class that day. (I know . . . you are shocked that any student would ever forget what you taught them. Try to contain yourself.)

- Make sure the written definition is in kid-friendly language!

STAGE 3
Providing Multiple Opportunities for Mastery

After you have taught students most of the essential vocabulary, it's time to bring back those Vocabulary Connection Cards and conduct an actual concept sort to help solidify their mastery. Refer back to Chapter 2 to refresh your memory about how to conduct a concept sort. Then try any of the following extensions and variations to take your students' learning even deeper.

Please note that *none* of these options requires any more preparation on your part! At the beginning of my career I thought the best lessons were those with carefully choreographed transitions, color-coded graphic organizers, and jazzy technology. Ten years later, I've learned that, though the bells and whistles are nice, they often put me on the computer cursing at Paint or burning my finger on the stupid laminator, when I should be enjoying valuable time with my own family. And most of the time, those extras don't elicit the huge increase in student learning I had hoped for anyway. What *does* create that increase is involving students in real conversations in which they can make real connections—and often that requires no planning at all!

Teach Your Sort

I conduct this activity in somewhat of a "fishbowl" format by having the entire class gather around each group's table. Some kids kneel down in front while others stand in the back, but we all huddle around one table to look and listen. I then quiz each group member on how their sort is arranged; for example, *Why did your group choose to place* fair *under the heading* Communism?

Anyone watching this part of the lesson would understand why teaching is an art, not a science. As I listen, I also guide the conversation in the right direction by correcting misconceptions and

Students explain their sort to the rest of the class.

highlighting important points while still encouraging the group members so they feel like the authorities on the topic. (And did I mention I am also keeping the two boys at the back from holding a dabbing contest, confiscating a cell phone, and monitoring the clock at the same time? BOOM!)

If the group had set aside any words they weren't sure about, I will often have the class help them find a place to put them. (Don't forget to take mental note of these words . . . formative assessment data!) After the group has finished their explanations, we give them a round of applause and rotate to the next group's sort.

Although this type of whole-class discussion can be exhausting, it is very valuable for a few reasons. First, it allows students to see multiple ways of sorting the same vocabulary words and to compare and contrast them. I praise them for thinking outside the box, and the next time students do a sort, I find they are even more creative in how they connect the words and even more thorough in their explanations. Second, it allows me to do a quick formative assessment of each student and see how well he or she understands the material. By the end of an hour, every single student has answered a question about the content or explained some piece of it to the class, and I am there to ask clarifying questions if necessary. Lastly, it allows me to build up each student's confidence by requiring him or her to speak to the whole class with me for support.

If, however, this 25-student gabfest isn't for you (or if you have *that* class that we all know will turn this activity into an impromptu mosh pit), there are several other great options for encouraging students to share and teach their sorts to their classmates.

Rotating Teachers

In this variation, inform students before the sort begins that they will all be responsible for "teaching" the completed sort to their classmates. In reality, you'll be choosing only one "teacher" from each group, but don't tell them that! A 2014 study from Washington University in St. Louis, Missouri (Everding), showed that just putting the expectation of having to teach information into students' heads prior to learning can increase their comprehension, so . . . *shhhhh!*

After all the groups have completed their sorts, have students elect one group member to teach their sort, or assign that role yourself. If you allow students to choose, remind them that this person should feel comfortable explaining the entire sort and answering questions about it. Next, while the "teachers" stay put, have all the groups rotate from their table to a neighboring one. The teacher then gets three minutes to teach the sort, and students get two minutes to ask the teacher questions about it. After the five minutes are up, have the groups rotate to a new table. Wrap up by asking students to share examples of sorts that impressed them or unique connections they saw as they rotated.

The downside to this strategy is that the "teachers" don't get exposed to the various ways of sorting. In addition, you may not be able to correct all misconceptions or check each student's comprehension. The upside is that smaller groups allow for deeper discussion and more time to ask questions. And usually students who are chosen, or volunteer, to be teachers are your higher-level kiddos who have already mastered the material and do a good job of communicating with their peers.

Add to the Sort

Another thing you can do before, after, or in place of sharing is to pass out blank cards and ask groups to add a few words of their choice to the sort. If you want to make it really challenging, have each group come up with some additional words then give them to another group to incorporate into their sort. Students will often choose words that clarify why they organized their cards the way they did or words that represent examples that stood out to them in class. This allows students to connect the words you have chosen to other words they have already internalized.

Alternatively, you can provide students with additional words you would like them to add to their sorts. I sometimes do this on the fly after all the groups have finished sharing their sorts. Often a certain word, phrase, or idea that isn't one of our Vocabulary Connection Cards will keep popping up in our discussions. At the end I might say, "What if I gave you another card that had *economic* on it? Where would you put that in your sort?"

Vocabulary Link-Ups

Another activity I love that highlights how essential terms are connected is Vocabulary Link-Ups. To start, have each student or group lay out their set of Vocabulary Connection Cards on the desk in front of them in no particular order. Begin the activity yourself by choosing a word, holding it up to show the class, and defining it. Instruct all

Students linking arms to show their words are connected

groups to flip over that word on their desk to show that it has already been used. Then ask for a volunteer to choose another word and explain its definition and how it is connected to your word. That student should bring his or her word card and stand next to you in front of the room to indicate that your words are "linked."

To further strengthen this connection, you can even have students link arms as they join the chain. (Although the older they are, the more likely this is to cause discomfort. Apparently linking arms is physically painful if you are a 7th-grade boy.) Once a student has added a word to the chain, all groups should flip over that card as well. Continue in this manner, allowing students to link up only to the ends of the chain, until all the words have been used or all students have had a turn. If you want to make this extra challenging, conclude the activity by seeing if the class can make the two ends of the chain connect!

I like to do this as a whole-class activity because it serves as a formative assessment, allowing me to see which students are struggling to make connections. Often, the last few students who are still sitting at the end of the activity will need help from you or their classmates to come up with a connection. To keep them from feeling pressured, you can casually walk by, point out a word that would work, and then "help" them through their explanation. In addition, you can provide some sort of reinforcement activity for them the following day.

This activity leads to some great class discussions and debates and gets students up and out of their seats! However, you can also have individual students do this on paper. I adapted the graphic organizer on page 45 from one shared with me by one of my awesome colleagues at Jackson Middle School, Tim Kluesner. It is more challenging than it appears! It works great as a homework assignment or as seatwork for students to complete in class.

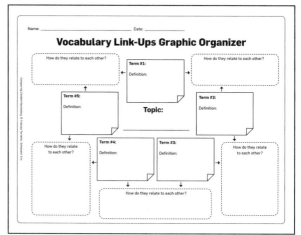

Vocabulary Link-Ups Graphic Organizer

Another variation of the link-up activity involves having students write their chosen words on long slips of paper and create a paper chain. Students can do this individually or in groups or pairs, then display the final product around the room or in the hall. If you are super ambitious, keep a class chain from each unit hanging on a bulletin board, and then at the end of the year challenge the class to find connections between the chains to create one long paper chain that connects all the concepts they've learned that year. It's a great visual to show continuity in the curriculum—something many students never really notice. I did this once in December, and we used the chains to decorate our classroom holiday tree! Free festive decorations for me, and a great time filler for those end-of-the-semester days of holiday parties and sugar highs!

Take It to the Board

If you want to get the whole class involved, but don't want to limit students to the linear connections required by Vocabulary Link-Ups, you can use your whiteboard or chalkboard to open things up a bit. Write each word on a sticky note and use the board as your "table." Conduct a regular concept sort, inviting each student to place one word at a time where he or she thinks it makes the most sense. Subsequent students can either change the placement of a classmate's word (giving a verbal explanation, of course) or place a new word. If you don't mind investing a little cash, you can even buy printable magnetic sheets, print the words on them, and cut them apart to create reusable, magnetic Vocabulary Connection Cards!

You can do this activity either after each group has completed a sort or in place of small-group sorting. The benefit is that it gives you more control over the discussion while allowing you to closely monitor the connections students are making. You can also easily assess which students are struggling and which words are the most challenging for your class. The downside is that some students are more likely to "check out" during whole-class activities than they would be if they were engaged with a smaller group of students. In addition, some students won't be as comfortable talking to the whole class and having to place their word in front of everyone, so make sure your students feel at ease with one another.

Divide and Conquer

I first used this approach with a class that had just the right combination of students that makes you want to go home, dig out your retirement portfolio, and calculate how much money you would need to retire by Christmas. Rather than starting them off in groups of four or five, pair off students and split one set of Vocabulary Connection Cards between the partners. Give the same instructions as you would to a group, but have each student sort his or her words individually—and silently. After giving them a sufficient amount of time to do this, instruct students to combine their sort with their partner's. This way each student hopefully has done a little independent thinking before joining forces. Once the pairs have finished their sorts, invite them to share their combined sort with the class or talk about them with a nearby pair.

I love how this strategy reduces the number of words for struggling students—keeping them from being overwhelmed—but also challenges them to take the connections they have already formed on their own and expand upon them with a partner. It stretches their brains and is great for both helping those quiet but thoughtful students to ease into group discussions and forcing Billy Blurter to think before he speaks. And it gives you a few precious minutes of silence. *happy sigh*

Share Your Struggle

The best and easiest way to use Vocabulary Connection Cards as a formative assessment is to ask students to share the words they are struggling with. After we've done a sort and discussed it using one of the strategies above, I often ask students at each table to choose one or two words they would still consider to be in their "Don't Know It" category and hold them up like a sign in front of them. Just by scanning the room I can easily see which words the class is struggling with and review them on the spot.

You can also group together students holding up the same word. Moving from group to group, you can reteach that specific topic or refer each group to a section from the reading piece that might help them tackle the word they are struggling with. Often I have students who see another classmate's struggle and volunteer a mental "trick" or mnemonic device that helps them remember that word. Let's face it—sometimes it takes a kid to teach a kid.

For this strategy to be successful, it is critical that your students feel safe putting their struggles out there. The last thing you want is for Billy Blurter to see someone's word and shout, "You don't know what *ecosystem* means? HA!" In *Visible Learning* (2012), Hattie says, "Expert teachers create classroom climates that welcome admission of errors; they achieve this by developing a climate of trust between teacher and student, and between student and student. The climate is one in which 'learning is cool,' worth engaging in, and everyone—teachers and students—is involved in the process of learning" (p. 26). Creating this optimal learning climate requires a bit of work, training students to be kind and constantly reminding them that not everyone masters information at the same pace. But I've found that taking the time to do this work with students pays dividends throughout the school year.

If you aren't sure how students will react to putting themselves out there, an easy alternative would be simply to have each student write his or her chosen word on a sticky note or exit slip and turn it in on the way out. This removes the social component but still collects the data you are so excited about recording! (Administrators? Observation? No?)

Connection Card Poker

This activity is really more like Uno, but calling it "poker" makes it seem a little bit more edgy. Playing in small groups, students deal the cards out evenly among themselves. The first player lays down a card and defines the word. The next player chooses a word from his own hand that connects to the first word played. Saying something like, "I'll see your *oil* and raise you *Persian Gulf*," the student sets down his card. The student must be able to explain the connection between the two words to his group mates' satisfaction; otherwise, he must take back his card and lose his turn. Play continues around the table until someone manages to play all his or her cards.

Dominoes

Create a set of dominoes on paper using the words from your Vocabulary Connection Cards. (Okay, so this one might require a *little* bit more work on your part.) You can create as many dominoes as you need and repeat the most important words multiple times, if necessary. Students play exactly as they would play a real game of dominoes, only instead of matching the same words together, they must match one word to another word by explaining how the two are linked. Their group mates must agree that the explanation provided makes sense before play continues.

This motivates students to give clear explanations and their group mates to listen carefully because they are usually trying to catch their opponents in a mistake! The typical rules of dominoes still apply. Players must draw from the pile if they can't play one of their dominoes, and the first person to play all his or her dominoes wins.

Technology ROCKS!

I'm not sure if you could detect the sarcasm in that heading, but it's definitely there. As you can probably guess from the focus of Vocabulary Connection Cards on human discussion and interaction, I am not a huge fan of online learning. I am the teacher who is more likely to pull out a tub of play dough than an iPad and who will die someday with my old-school paper grade book still clutched to my chest. But I won't deny that as instructional technology has progressed, I have been impressed with some of the amazing tools out there, and even I occasionally hold my breath and jump into the deep end of the technology pool. (I've even done a lesson with virtual-reality headsets . . . Yay, me!) So, if cutting out paper Vocabulary Connection Cards is not for you, never fear! There are several ways to take concept sorting into the digital world.

- On both Google Docs (using Insert > Drawing…) and Google Slides you can create textboxes and type your words in them. Students can then click and drag the textboxes to sort them on the screen. This works great in a whole-class setting, but you can also share the files with students via email or whatever Learning Management System (LMS) your school prefers, then have them save and submit their finished sorts back to you. Google is by nature very user-friendly and widely used by parents and students. And because Google allows live editing by multiple collaborators, you could potentially have an entire class of students engaged in a single sort at the same time without ever leaving their seats!

  The downside is that students may need to log in to their own Google account to save and send the file while maintaining formatting. And although the live editing feature of Google is cool, there is some learning curve with how to share files so as to avoid students editing your original document.

- Another alternative is to use traditional word processing software, such as Microsoft Word or even PowerPoint, to create concept sorts that you can project and manipulate on a screen. As with Google Docs and Slides, simply insert textboxes with your words typed in them. Or you can utilize SMART Board software, if you are lucky enough to have one of those bad boys in your room!

- A quick online search for "digital word sorts" will turn up numerous websites that allow you to create your own word sorts. Unfortunately, many of them are structured for those elementary closed sorts that focus on spelling and word parts (e.g., sorting words by the blends *th* and *ch*). Because Vocabulary Connection Cards utilize open sorting, in which there are multiple correct ways to organize the words, it requires software that allows the same. SpunkyEnglish.com has a free tool called

Magnet Maker, which works well. Triptico Plus (www.tripticoplus.com) allows you to customize a plethora of educational tools, including word sorts, for an annual subscription fee. Or, if your school uses iPads, use the Post-It® Plus app (by the makers of Post-It Notes) to take a picture of your Vocabulary Connection Cards and turn them into moveable, digital sticky notes!

Just don't forget that the magic of Vocabulary Connection Cards is in the conversations students have while working on their sorts. If going digital helps keep your students actively engaged while still allowing them to have those conversations, then by all means, click away! But if moving Connection Cards to a screen takes away from that dynamic, then head back to the printer and that good ol' paper cutter! Instructional technology incorporated simply because it looks cool or follows some current trend isn't worth the sacrifice.

Combining Units

One last way to extend the learning is to combine two sets of Vocabulary Connection Cards from adjoining units. For example, in our world history curriculum, Unit 3 is Ancient Greece and Unit 4 is Ancient Rome. After we have finished both units, I create a set of Vocabulary Connection Cards that combines key elements that are common between the two. For example, while Greece was the birthplace of democracy, Rome took it a step further and created a republic. By including both those words, as well as some evaluative terms, such as *best*, *different*, or *similar*, you can help students recognize broader themes across the curriculum or even across content areas.

Stage 3 Wrap-Up

With Vocabulary Connection Cards, the options and variations are limited only by your imagination. I frequently find myself tweaking my plan as I go and even differentiating from one hour to the next, all while having had to prepare only one simple activity! I have no doubt that if you try it, you will find yourself creating even more new ways to use this activity to benefit your students.

Name: _____

Date: _____

Vocabulary Link-Ups Graphic Organizer

Topic:

Term #1:

Definition:

How do they relate to each other?

Term #2:

Definition:

How do they relate to each other?

Term #3:

Definition:

How do they relate to each other?

Term #4:

Definition:

How do they relate to each other?

Term #5:

Definition:

How do they relate to each other?

Chapter Four

The Importance of Writing

When I was a student, we were often required to use our newly learned vocabulary words in a sentence. We would always go above and beyond and come up with literary masterpieces, such as, "*Economics* is interesting." (Don't roll your eyes . . . you know you did it too.)

We all know that getting students to use new words in their writing is critical. The authors of *Content-Area Writing: Every Teacher's Guide* (Daniels, Zemelman & Steineke, 2007) call this type of writing outside the ELA classroom "writing to learn" (p. 20)—it helps solidify the words in students' brains and requires them to clearly articulate the connections between words. When we write to learn, "we are using writing to find out what's inside our heads, to dump ideas down on a page so we can play with them, move them around, make connections, figure out what's important, cross some out, and highlight others. In other words, we are thinking" (p. 21).

However, we all know it can be a challenge to find time to incorporate legitimate writing assignments into our curriculum, let alone find the time to grade them. Grading essays sucks. (Wait . . . did I just say that out loud?)

I've found that the answer lies in shorter, more frequent written assignments that I can use quickly to gauge student understanding without taking the time to actually grade them. You read that right. Don't grade them. If this makes you a bit nervous, don't worry. Daniels et al., got your back. They assure us that "the intensive correction of student papers does not work; it has never worked and it never will work. Kids' writing does not improve when teachers cover their papers with corrections, no matter how scrupulous and generous that type of feedback may seem" (p. 24). (I seriously need to start them a fan club!) Remember, the benefit of writing for students comes from *their* thinking and writing the words on paper, not on your grading of that work. It can be just as effective to read through their answers, choose a few exceptional ones to share with the class, and spend some time analyzing them together as it would have been for you to spend hours grading and writing feedback on 120 essays.

In addition, as a non-ELA teacher, your focus is on *what* students say, much more than *how* they say it. While it might be quick and easy to correct their spelling or grammar with a red pen, correcting their misuse or misunderstanding of the word *erosion* takes a lot more time and energy. You would basically have to write a little mini-lesson in the margin! In other words, this type of feedback can be difficult and time-consuming to communicate on paper, but easily tackled in a lecture or class discussion.

So what does this have to do with Vocabulary Connection Cards?

Vocabulary words are the building blocks of good writing. Vocabulary Connection Cards lend themselves quite well to various writing prompts and activities because they serve as a word bank from which students can draw for any writing assignment. These words focus students' attention on important concepts while still requiring them to demonstrate their own level of understanding. In addition, writing is a great way to help students begin to transfer the deeper-level critical-thinking skills they've developed with Connection Cards into a more concrete and academic form. Below are a few ideas for how to use Connection Cards to add writing to your instruction.

Remember, these aren't meant to be graded with a rubric or pored over with a red pen. Collect them as a quick ticket-out-the-door, invite students to share them in class, or simply give them a once over while you watch students work. Any of these methods will get you the formative assessment data you need, while sparing you hours of grading. You're welcome!

Summary

Choose five words from the set of Vocabulary Connection Cards for your current unit of study. If you like to live dangerously, invite a student to choose them! Place these words on the board where everyone can see them. Instruct students to write a summary of what they have learned so far, being sure to include and underline those five words. I like to do this as a ticket-out-the-door to check for understanding quickly and efficiently. A summary makes it fairly difficult for students to pull an "*Economics* is interesting" stunt, and it very rarely stretches more than one paragraph in length. Reading through the summaries quickly, I can get a good sense of which content needs to be revisited.

Story

If you're feeling a little more creative, give students a story prompt that lends itself to the topic being studied and challenge them to finish the story using as many words from their Vocabulary Connection Cards as possible.

For example, for a unit on magnetism you could give students this prompt:

> *Earth is being attacked by aliens. You are one of the few people left to fight back. While you and some fellow rebels are taking cover in an abandoned warehouse, a scientist with your group points out that the alien ships appear to have large magnets mounted on their landing gear. Just then, one of the ships discovers your hiding spot. What happens next?*

Don't forget to stipulate that students must incorporate a certain number of Vocabulary Connection Card words into their story and show their meanings. Otherwise, you'll just be reading a bunch of middle-school variations of *Men in Black* and *Independence Day*. (Sounds pretty entertaining, I know, but you are a teacher. Stay focused!)

R.A.F.T.

This strategy, developed by Carol Minnick Santa (1988), is a really fun way to incorporate writing into any content area and to allow students to do some creative thinking. Students choose (or may be assigned) a Role, Audience, Format, and Topic to write about. See below for one I created for a unit on Ancient Rome.

Of course, this can be done without Vocabulary Connection Cards, but challenging students to incorporate as many words from the cards as they can into their R.A.F.T. helps focus their writing on the content they need to master and allows you to use their finished product as a formative check of their understanding of each concept.

Ancient Rome R.A.F.T.

ROLE	AUDIENCE	FORMAT	TOPIC
Julius Caesar	Roman Senate	speech	Convince them to make you dictator for life, now that you have defeated Pompeii
Hadrian	Legionnaires at the Northern Border	building plans	Explain why you want them to build the wall, and give them instructions on how to do it
Christian citizen of Rome	A friend in another Roman province	letter	React to Constantine's new law that Christianity is legal across the Empire
Brutus	Self	diary/journal	Reflect on the assassination of your friend, Julius Caesar
Hannibal	His troops as they cross the Alps	speech	Encourage and motivate soldiers to continue the fight against Rome
Foreign visitor to Rome	A friend from your homeland	letter	Explain how the Republic is different from your own King and how it works. Do you like it? Why or why not?
Plebeian	Other Roman Plebeians	speech	Persuade them to join you in going on strike to get more say in the Roman government

Have students incorporate as many vocabulary words into their R.A.F.T. to help focus their writing.

Dialogue

Create a fictional situation in which two characters would be discussing the topics covered in the unit—the more fantastical, the better! For example, during a unit on the scientific method, ask students to pretend to be two survivors of the zombie apocalypse arguing over the best zombie deterrent . . . or a dragon and a chicken discussing the fastest way to hatch an egg . . . or Dr. Frankenstein and Igor wondering how to proceed with their latest experiment. Be creative! Have students work in pairs and assume the roles of the two characters and write a dialogue. The challenge is that each time they speak, they must include one Vocabulary Connection Card word in their dialogue, while still keeping the conversation logical. Once a word is used, it cannot be chosen again. If you want to make it harder, make them choose a word without looking. Challenge students to carry on their conversation, either verbally or in writing, until all the words have been incorporated. Then you can collect and read the dialogues, or, if you really want to have some fun, have students perform them in front of the class!

Fill in the Blanks

Have students write a short fill-in-the-blanks story or summary in which the Vocabulary Connection Cards are the missing words. Remind them that in order for someone to be able to complete their fill-in-the-blank, it must have enough "clues" that identify the correct missing word. Then have students trade stories with a partner and, using the Vocabulary Connection Cards as their word bank, fill in the missing words. Alternatively, you can complete one together as a class.

Write Your Own Test Questions

Have students choose a card at random and write a possible test question that either includes the word or has that word as the correct answer. Then have students trade questions with a partner and answer them as a practice quiz. Or, if you're really brave, select some of their questions to include in an actual test. This will elicit even better questions the next time you do it as students like to compete to see if their questions show up on test day.

Chapter Wrap-Up

- Once you have made Vocabulary Connection Cards a regular part of your instructional lineup, incorporate these simple writing activities as a natural next step.

- Short writing assignments help students begin to organize their thoughts in an academic way, while allowing you to more accurately evaluate each student's mastery.

- Sharing completed writing assignments with the class or with a partner substitutes for grading hours of essays, but still reaps rewards for students.

Chapter Five

Making Connections at Home

When my oldest child started kindergarten, I was amazed and perplexed that I started receiving text messages from her teacher. Mind you, these were not blanket reminder texts generated by some computer program, but personal texts from her teacher to me, saying things like, "Tessa was a little upset at recess today and said her stomach hurt. She laid down in the nurse's office for a bit, and she seems fine now. Just wanted to let you know!" or "Here's a pic of our math lab activity today! Tessa loved it!" At our first parent-teacher conference I gushed about how amazing it was and wondered how she possibly found the time for such consistent, personal communication. She looked a little confused and said, "Well, I only have 14 students." Whoa. Suddenly I was looking at the world upside down and through the rose-colored glasses of a perennially cheerful and sweet-natured elementary school teacher. It was weird.

While I understand that very few elementary school teachers are blessed with classes of only 14, even larger classes of 25 to 30 are a far cry from the 125 to 150 tween-age souls that many middle school teachers wrangle on a daily basis. What's more, middle school is often the first time students have multiple teachers in a day AND the first time responsibility for things like organization, homework completion, and scheduling begins to shift away from the parents and onto the students. The combination of these factors makes consistent parent-teacher communication much more challenging.

I've also noticed that many parents of middle-school students have an equally hard time with this transition. They struggle to figure out just how involved they should be in their student's school life. Should they help with his homework? Should they call the teacher about that low grade? Or should they take a step back and let their child start being responsible for some of this on her own?

Of course, each student is different, and the real answer is probably somewhere in the middle. But in the area of studying for tests and quizzes, middle school is the age where students should start learning to study on their own rather than relying exclusively on mom or dad to quiz them or go over notes with them. Vocabulary Connection Cards are a great way to guide students and parents in the right direction.

At the end of a unit I often give each student his or her own set of Vocabulary Connection Cards to take home. This can be much smaller than a regular set. Simply create a table in a Word document and type the words as large as you can while still keeping them all on one page. Then make enough photocopies on brightly colored cardstock and pass them out. Have students cut apart their cards and place them in a small envelope to take home. There are several ways students and parents can use them to study, many of which mirror activities presented in Chapter 3. Here are some of my favorites.

Schooling the Parents

This is by far my favorite home review strategy—and my students' favorite too! After passing out the student sets of Vocabulary Connection Cards, I tell the class, "Tonight we're going to see just how smart your parents are!" Having already done at least one concept sort with me in class, students know how it works, so I tell them to task their parents (or older brothers or sisters) with sorting the words themselves. Then students get to critique their parents' explanations, pointing out all their mistakes and misconceptions. As you can imagine, kids love this! What middle schooler doesn't love to prove his or her parents wrong or at the very least argue with them? I have had several parents tell me they learned a lot from their child doing this activity, and even more students tell me how much fun they had "schooling" their parents!

This method of studying and reviewing hits the perfect blend of student accountability and parent support. It puts students in the role of expert, encouraging them to take responsibility for the learning, but it involves parents more extensively than just, "Here, Mom, can you quiz me on these definitions?"

It also shows parents the depth of comprehension we are aiming for. One of the biggest questions I get from parents fresh out of an elementary setting is, "Do you give out study guides?" And more often than not, the type of study guide they expect is a list of terms and definitions they can quiz their child on the night before the test. I can't fault them for their expectations, especially since that is precisely the type of assessments I was given in school as well, and at an elementary level, some rote memorization is common. However, I like to assign the Vocabulary Connection Cards as a study tool at home to illustrate to parents that in the upper grades a deeper level of comprehension will be required.

Perhaps even more importantly, I have seen Connection Cards prompt real connections and conversations between pre-teens and their parents at a time in their lives when communication between them could not be more important—and more volatile! I think parents and students alike appreciate the chance to do something together besides argue about dating or how much makeup is too much. I once had a parent tell me that Connection Cards had sparked an hour-long family dinner table discussion about capitalism, communism, socialism, and current political issues connected to those topics. She thanked me and commented, "I really enjoyed it . . . and I was surprised at how much Logan knew!"

Unit Preview

Just as in the classroom, Vocabulary Connection Cards can be beneficial to send home *before* learning begins. Hooking parents at the beginning of a new unit of study is a widely underutilized strategy for helping students succeed. In middle school, I hear from parents all the time that they have no idea what's going on at school because "my kids never tell me anything!" Giving them a heads-up before a unit starts makes them much more likely to ask their child specifically about that topic and to help keep her on track with homework and studying. Of course, a simple email would do the trick, but where's the fun in that? Instead, give students a set of Vocabulary Connection Cards to take home and have them work with their parents to write one sentence describing what they think they will learn in the upcoming unit. Have them return the cards with their statement the following day. (This is even cooler if students haven't seen the cards beforehand, but I have never found the time to cut apart and stuff 120 sets of Connection Cards into envelopes myself. If you are more ambitious than me or if you have a small army of minions, go for it!)

Alternatively, you could send home the title or topic of the unit and ask parents and students to come up with a list of key vocabulary terms they think might be critical to learning about that topic. This allows parents to do a little bit of the front-loading of prior knowledge for you . . . and gets them invested in their kid's learning early in the unit.

In both approaches described above, you can present the task as a challenge or a mystery to be solved. Students and parents alike will be excited to see if they were correct in their guesses. The following day students will go home, eager to tell their parents if they were right and hopefully share whatever other information they learned in class that day. Natural parent engagement achieved . . . and you didn't even have to make a phone call!

Bonus on the Back

If you plan to send these Vocabulary Connection Cards home early in a unit rather than at the end, or if you just want to provide a little more support for struggling learners, it may be helpful to have students write the definition of each key term on the back of its card. This way parents and students can still sort the Vocabulary Connection Cards, but if there is any disagreement or uncertainty about a term, they can simply flip the card to reveal its definition. This allows mom and dad to save face when they can't immediately recall the definition of *mitochondria*. Let's face it, no one wants to play "Are You Smarter Than a 5th Grader?" with their own fifth grader! (My daughter is going into 2nd grade, and I can tell you there have already been several times when she asked me for help with her homework, and I was stumped. It's not a good feeling.) Providing those definitions will help parents who may not feel confident about the material and allow them to participate constructively in study time— making it much more likely that they will do so now and in the future. It also prevents an overly confident student from "teaching" his parents all the wrong information, and thereby studying the wrong stuff! It allows the parent who is sitting there thinking, "Wait a minute . . . I don't think that sounds right . . ." to double check the information without digging out old textbooks or consulting the Internet. "Alexa, what's an *improper fraction* again?"

If you do choose to have students include definitions, one word of caution. Because flashcards are such a commonly used study tool for memorization, parents are bound to see the Vocabulary Connection Cards with the definitions written on the back and think, "Flashcards!" Students may become frustrated trying to explain the idea of a concept sort to their parents, while many parents will be adamant that their students are supposed to simply memorize the definitions. To avoid this confusion, consider sending parents a note or email, like the one on page 55, explaining how concept sorts work. You might even include a photo of a sort completed in class. As the year goes on and parents become more familiar with the activity, an explanation won't be necessary.

Parents Add to the Sort

In Chapter 3, I suggested giving students blank slips of paper on which to write words to add to their sort. Once parents are used to the idea of Vocabulary Connection Cards, you might take it a step further and send home a couple of blank cards for them to add words to the sort. Again, this will undoubtedly lead to a learning conversation between students and parents, who might discuss words that weren't covered in class. Maybe mom or dad will follow up the next day to see what you thought of the words they added. (Make sure to ask students to share those words with you, by the way. It's a great bell-ringer activity!) Regardless of whether the words are pertinent to your lesson, students and parents are having learning conversations. Mission accomplished!

Parent Homework

When I was a student, several of my teachers offered extra credit if my mom or dad signed my study guide. While I know attitudes toward extra credit vary (my district is against it), encouraging students and parents to interact with each other over content is never a bad thing! Signatures are SO old school, but a more modern take might involve asking parents to text or email you a photo of their completed sort. Or, if you allow students to have cell phones at school, simply ask them to show you a photo of their sort. If you are more tech-savvy than me, you could even ask for videos of them explaining their connections! Offer a small prize for any student whose parent submits a photo or video—it's amazing what kids will do for a Jolly Rancher! You can also offer to share some of the photos with the class! Students get a kick out of their parents' work being shared, and the novelty acts as its own "extra credit."

If you feel that students and parents have progressed to a point where a simple sort is too easy, you could also send home one of the writing activities described in Chapter 4 as a parent-student assignment. Of course, no grades need be taken. (In my classroom, I don't penalize students who aren't able to finish the assignment.) You can share the completed writing pieces with the class as an interesting discussion starter or wrap-up activity. Even if only a handful of parents participate, it is a quick and easy way to extend the learning beyond the classroom.

Peer Study Groups

Even without parent involvement, Vocabulary Connection Cards can be a great study tool. I encourage my students to use their cards to complete a concept sort with a partner or a small group in study hall, or even on their own at home before an upcoming test or quiz. While I may not be there to guide their discussion, the act of organizing and thinking about the words is a great way for students to review at the end of a unit. I have even caught students in the cafeteria before school playing Poker or Vocabulary Link-Ups with their friends before a test—completely unprompted!

Think about the last study guide you sent home, and imagine what your students looked like as they used it to study. More than likely, you picture them sitting and staring at the paper silently or maybe having a friend quiz them over memorized definitions. Simply providing a manipulative, like Vocabulary Connection Cards, for students to interact with makes them much more likely to engage actively with the content. And because Connection Cards include those supporting words, such as *fair, compare,* and *best,* they require students to make deeper connections beyond memorizing definitions.

Chapter Wrap-Up

Keeping the lines of communication open between school and home is always a challenge. Let's face it . . . at the end of a long day, making parent phone calls is not what most teachers are looking forward to! (We'd rather go home, put on sweats, and order Chinese food . . . or maybe that's just me?) Oftentimes, parents feel the same way, and calling or emailing school gets pushed further and further down their to-do list. Vocabulary Connection Cards are a flexible, family-friendly way to help parents keep tabs on what's happening in the classroom, while also encouraging their angst-filled middle schooler to have a real conversation with them. That simple envelope full of words will not only improve student comprehension and build positive study habits—it will also build positive relationships. Win-win!

Dear Parents:

Tonight your student will be challenging you to show what YOU know about our current unit on
_____ ! Your child will have an envelope with a set of 25 to 35 cards containing key vocabulary words from our current unit. In our classroom, we call them Vocabulary Connection Cards. Here is your mission, should you choose to accept it:

1. Find a large, flat area to work on. (The kitchen table or countertop works great!)

2. Empty the envelope onto the table and lay out the cards face up.

3. Sort or organize the cards in any way you think makes sense, based on what you know about the words. (Your child may watch but not help you yet!) You may choose to put the words into groups or categories based on similarities and differences, arrange them in chronological order, pair causes with effects, and so on. Be creative!

    For example, in this sample sort about farms, the words show a progression of events: The *barn* is where we store the *tractor*, which we use to *grow corn*, which feeds the *pig*.

    Another equally correct way to sort might be to group equipment farmers use and products they grow, like this:

    The goal is simply to show the connections you see between the words by moving them around on the table. There are MANY correct ways to do this!

4. When you are finished, explain to your child why you sorted the cards the way you did. See whether or not your child agrees with your understanding of the words. You never know, your student may be able to teach you something! Feel free to work together to make changes to your sort.

5. If you are able, please snap a photo of your completed sort and send it to me at
    _____ so we can share it with the class! Feel free to include any questions you and your child may have.

Have fun, and happy sorting!

_____
Teacher's signature

Sample Lists and Tips for Each Content Area

Vocabulary Connection Cards are invaluable for teaching vocabulary in any subject, including math, science, social studies, and a broad range of elective classes. As I'm sure you are aware, each content area is totally unique, and consequently there are some things to keep in mind that are unique to each content setting.

The following pages offer some tips to consider in each of the three core content-heavy areas of math, science, and social studies, as well as sample word and picture cards for some common units of study in each—just to get you started! Use these cards as a jumping-off point to create your own Vocabulary Connection Cards. As I mentioned in Chapter 2, they don't have to be fancy; a document with 48-point font and a pair of scissors will work just fine! Please note that I have included more than the 25 to 35 words you will need, so choose the words that match your unit and feel free to skip or add words as necessary. If you choose to include pictures in your sort, Google Images is a great resource. Just make sure to choose pictures that will photocopy well, as you will likely be making multiple sets of cards.

Also, depending on the vertical alignment of your district's curriculum, some of the "known" words I included may or may not be familiar to your students. Remember, it's not all that important to determine whether each word is new, known, or supporting—as long as you have included at least a few of each.

MATH

Since students are often unfamiliar with the concept of discussion in math, it might be best to scale back the number of Vocabulary Connection Cards you use to start. You might present students with six or seven words and pictures as a starter, or complete the first sort together as a class.

Model, model, model. Students aren't used to talking about math because they aren't used to seeing their teachers talk about it! The first few times you ask them to do a concept sort will likely be rough unless you model it for them first. Use sticky notes or magnets (see "Take It to the Board," page 41) and sort the words yourself on the board, thinking out loud as you go. Or using a projector, you can complete a mini-sort on your desk and explain why you chose to place each word where you did.

I've found pictures are very helpful to include in math sorts. Look for pictures of real-world applications of the concept being taught or for a photo that could represent an abstract concept. For example, I might include a picture like this, at right, in a word sort about calculating volume. Of course, the goal would be for students to recognize that a shipping company, such as FedEx, would need to know the volume of its trucks in order to determine how many packages they can carry. And if students don't get that connection, then what a great teachable moment!

Include common math symbols or even sample math problems,

Double trailer truck

when appropriate. However, avoid turning this into a glorified matching game in which students simply match equations with answers, fractions with decimal equivalents, and so on. Keep the focus on the how and why behind the math, not the calculations themselves.

PLACE VALUE

standard form	word form	place value
<	>	round
expanded form	millions	hundred thousands
ten thousands	thousands	hundreds
tens	ones	place value chart
digit	=	greater than
less than	equal to	3,000
40,0000	700,000	200

PLACE VALUE

80	3	489,037
26,875	231	7,937
comma	bigger	smaller
least	greatest	order
compare	contest	split
difference	move	

PLACE VALUE

Place Value

Millions	Hundred Thousands	Ten Thousands	Thousands	Hundreds	Tens	Ones
1	5	6	4	7	9	8

one million, five hundred sixty-four thousand, seven hundred ninety-eight

Write your number here:

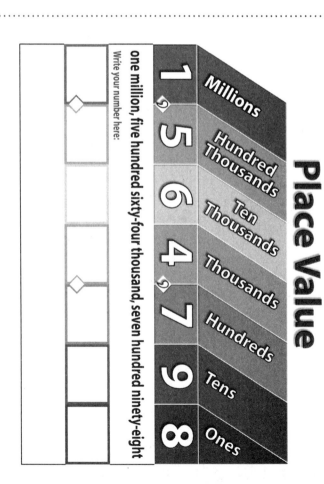

FRACTIONS

fraction	composite	prime
numerator	denominator	equivalent
improper	mixed number	simplest form
common	factor	multiple
prime factorization	reduce	least common denominator (LCD)
least common multiple (LCM)	unit fraction	equal
part	whole	divide
$\dfrac{5}{2}$	$\dfrac{3}{4}$	$3\dfrac{1}{3}$

FRACTIONS

greatest	least	compare
share	top	bottom
different	same	can
cannot	decimal	multiply
like	unlike	whole number

FRACTIONS

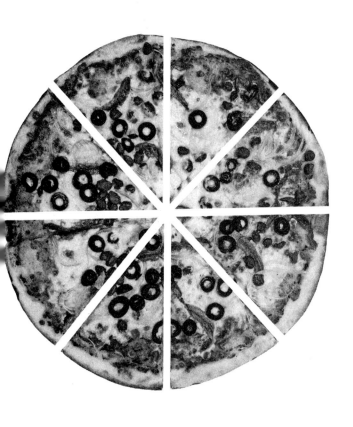

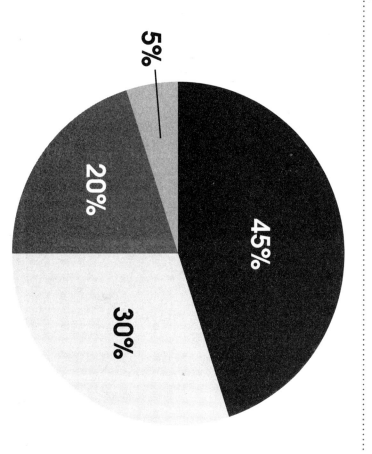

5%

20%

45%

30%

PERIMETER, AREA, AND VOLUME

area	volume	perimeter
length	width	height
unit square	square units	cubic units
cube	rectangular prism	m^3
m^2	$V = l \times w \times h$	$V = b \times h$
base	surface area	total
sides	$=$	$\times$
rectangle	square	measure

PERIMETER, AREA, AND VOLUME

add	edge	inside
outside	calculate	all
cover	around	fill
space	largest	

PERIMETER, AREA, AND VOLUME

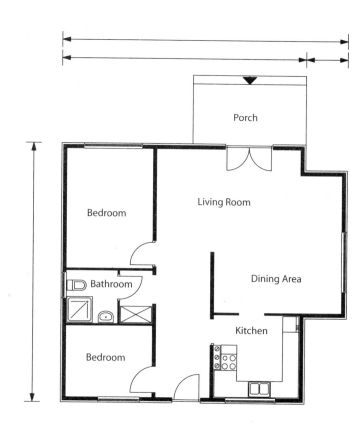

SOLVING EQUATIONS

equation	variable	inverse
operations	property	equality
like terms	distributive	identity
solution	expand	expression
+	−	=
×	÷	combine
subtraction	multiplication	division
addition	order	fractions

SOLVING EQUATIONS

equals	check	always
same	alone	isolate
opposite	both	true
false	replace	all

SOLVING EQUATIONS

"Just a darn minute — yesterday you said that X equals **two**!"

$$x + 2 = 5$$
$$x = 3$$

PERCENT

percent	$500, 3.5%, 6 years	principal
simple interest	rate	I = prt
total cost	15% of 57	67 to 78
percent of change	proportion	ratio
tip	sales tax	fraction
decimal	part	time
whole	price	100
equation	÷	%

PERCENT

=	×	_____
denominator	numerator	always
choice	compare	all
solve	different	same
before	after	

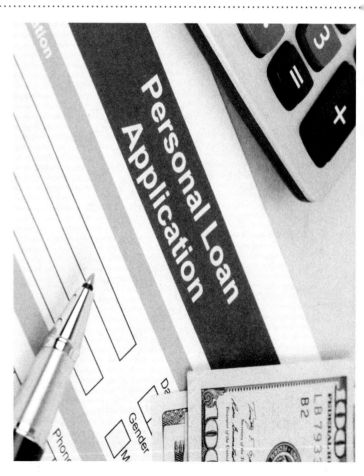

SCIENCE

Science lends itself to Vocabulary Connection Cards because of the wealth of diagrams, flow charts, and relationships among organisms and systems, which are already graphic in nature. But be careful not to choose words and pictures that make one method of sorting too obvious. For example, if your Connection Cards include only the words *mammals, amphibians, reptiles, invertebrates, fish,* and *birds,* and then lots of examples of each, such as *human, catfish, giraffe, sparrow,* and so on, then your students are sure to simply categorize the animals by type. But if you include words like *water, warm, first, evolution, most,* and *vertebrates,* among others, their depth of knowledge improves tremendously.

Pictures and symbols are also great to include in a science sort. You can add diagrams, graphs, and any other visual elements you think will get students' brains humming.

Don't forget to connect it to real life! A photo of a greenhouse for photosynthesis or of a bottle of hand sanitizer for a unit on diseases will do the trick.

SCIENTIFIC METHOD

inquiry	accuracy	control group
data	evidence	experiment
hypothesis	inference	observation
precision	independent	investigation
empirically	random sample	quantitative
qualitative	prediction	question
collect	conclusion	measurements
results	opinion	record

SCIENTIFIC METHOD

important	most	best
always	never	change
effect	cause	expect
surprise	bias	procedure
variable	dependent	

SCIENTIFIC METHOD

Fresh water

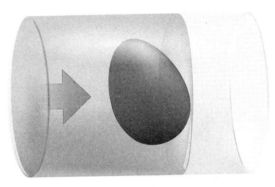

Salt water

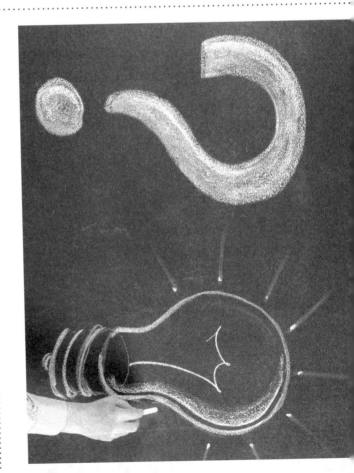

MAGNETISM

magnetic field	atoms	protons
ferromagnetic	magnetism	poles
solar wind	elements	magnetosphere
nucleus	aurora	physical
magnet	electrons	magnetic domain
iron	geographic	magnetic
declination	attract	repel
electricity	sun	north

MAGNETISM

south	positive	negative
permanent	temporary	weak
strong	observe	together
apart	never	always
useful	push	pull
cause	effect	

MAGNETISM

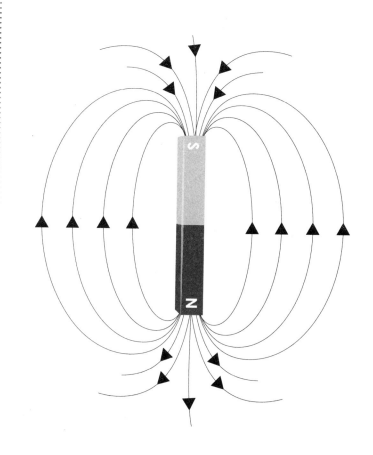

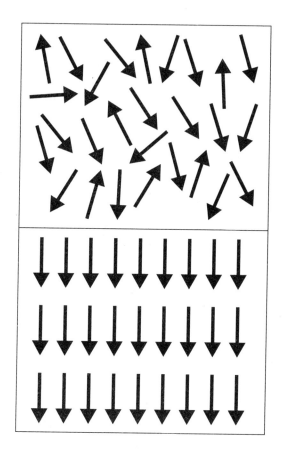

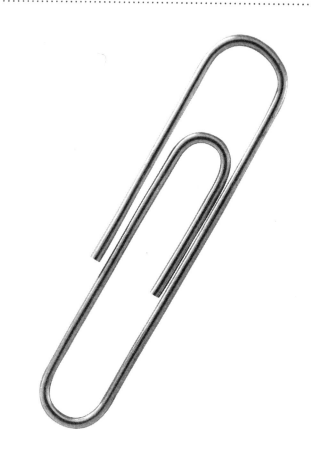

THE EARTH

crust	mantle	outer core
inner core	magnetic field	molten
tectonic plates	continental drift	faults
divergent boundary	convergent boundary	transform boundary
stress	tension	compression
shearing	strike-slip	magma
temperature	pressure	rock
metal	liquid	movement

THE EARTH

volcanoes	mountains	trenches
earthquakes	normal	reverse
thick	thin	layers
apart	together	collide
opposite	many	fast
slow	cause	effect
break	heat	solid

THE EARTH

PANGAEA

Tethys ocean

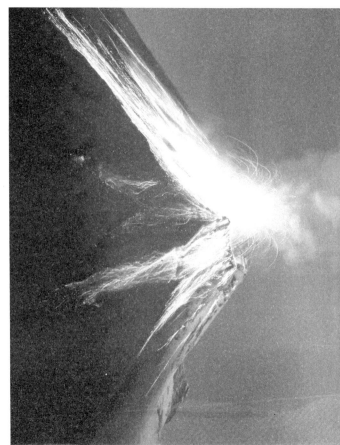

ENERGY

energy	sound	kinetic
light	potential	gravitational
chemical	elastic	vibrations
charged	electromagnetic	joules
electrical	thermal	mechanical
nuclear	motion	change
transfer	stored	heat
waves	power	released

ENERGY

cause	effect	increase
decrease	useful	feel
see	hear	possible
dangerous	safe	

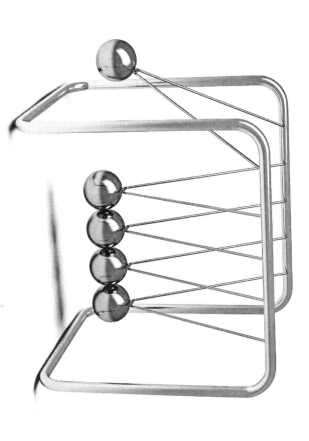

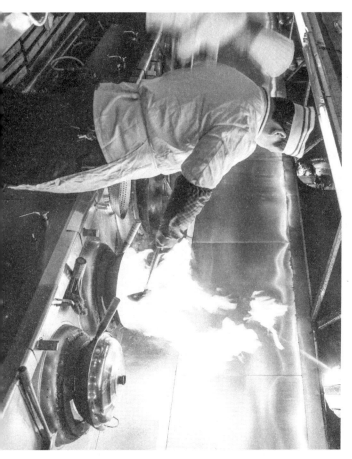

MATTER

mass	matter	atom
molecule	elements	nonmetals
semimetals	plasma	protons
neutrons	electrons	compounds
nucleus	state	evaporation
condensation	gases	solids
liquids	types	metals
properties	color	volume

MATTER

temperature	texture	shape
freeze	melt	space
many	different	alike
two	connect	always
smallest	close	far
change	high	low
hard	fill	

MATTER

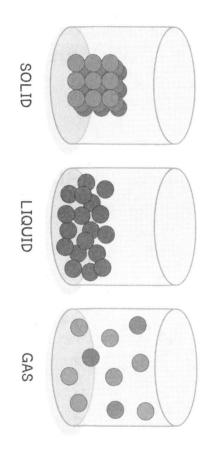

SOLID

LIQUID

GAS

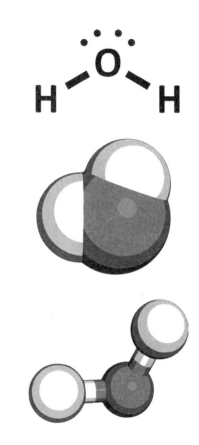

PERIODIC TABLE OF THE ELEMENTS

SOCIAL STUDIES

Of course, I may be partial, but I think social studies is the content area where Vocabulary Connection Cards really shine. Social studies is, by nature, a subject of debate, evaluation, discussion, and choices. It is also a part of nearly every other content area. We learn the history of scientific discoveries and debate their ethics. We use math and statistics to evaluate social trends and direct policy decisions. And subjects such as art, music, and technology undoubtedly have made a huge impact on our history and our culture. Because of all these reasons, there are so many connections to be made!

While pictures can occasionally be useful, often the words themselves, particularly the non-content–specific words that require students to make judgments, prompt the deepest, most meaningful discussions. Don't be tempted to replace a critical vocabulary word with a picture of the same. For example, I once created a set of Connection Cards on Ancient Greece that contained the picture at top right.

My students were all able to match it with the words *Greece* and *Aegean Sea* during the concept sort, but when it came time to take the assessment, many of them did not know its name! (It's a *trireme*, non-history folks.) I had made the mistake of using a picture in place of a critical vocabulary word.

If you really feel that a visual would get kids engaged, or if you want to provide extra support for special-needs students, you may consider including the word itself on the picture card, like this one at bottom right.

TRIREME

In social studies, it is extra important to include words that require students to make judgments or state their opinions, whenever possible. There are so many great opportunities for this in social studies, and there is no better way to help students clarify their thinking than to ask them to defend their opinions. Toss in some words such as *best, never, should, important, fair, change,* or *power* and see what your students do with them. I guarantee they can and will surprise you!

MAP SKILLS

legend	key	political
physical	relief	thematic
special purpose	compass	scale
projection	latitude	longitude
equator	prime meridian	hemisphere
degrees	elevation	north
south	east	west
cities	countries	mountains

MAP SKILLS

rivers	distance	grid
North Pole	South Pole	best
same	different	locate
tools	divide	vertical
horizontal	measure	3-D
2-D		

MAP SKILLS

1 inch represents 3000 miles

0
3000
6000
9000 miles

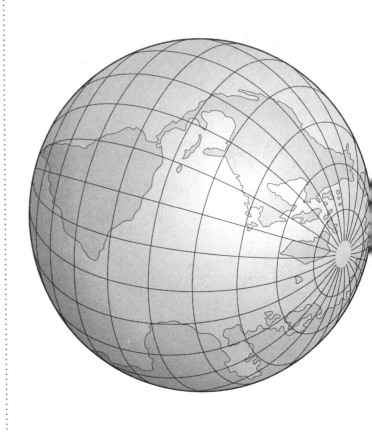

U.S. GOVERNMENT

legislative	judicial	executive
checks and balances	Senate	House of Representatives
Speaker of the House	veto	Supreme Court
Congress	unconstitutional	political party
Representatives	Senators	term
nomination	bill	law
President	Vice President	government
democracy	vote	republic

U.S. GOVERNMENT

Republicans	Democrats	debate
power	3	9
2	100	435
election	years	4
6	limit	states
positive	negative	compromise
believe	share	divide
protect	decide	better

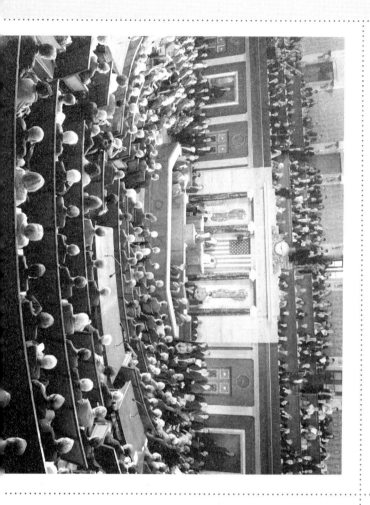

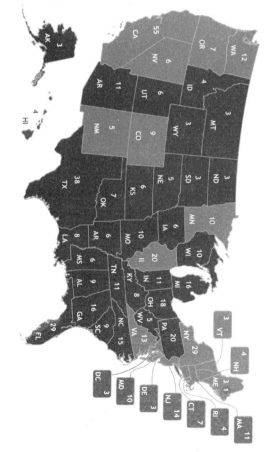

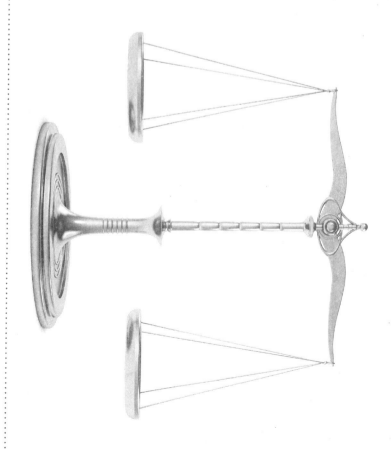

ROAD TO THE AMERICAN REVOLUTION

King George III	Sugar Act	tyranny
Stamp Act	Patrick Henry	Townshend Acts
boycott	Boston Massacre	John Adams
Patriot	Continental Congress	Lexington and Concord
Paul Revere	Intolerable Acts	Loyalist
Bunker Hill	Benjamin Franklin	*Common Sense*
Thomas Jefferson	Declaration of Independence	militia
George Washington	colonies	Great Britain

ROAD TO THE AMERICAN REVOLUTION

tea	Philadelphia	liberty
taxes	independent	New York
east	fair	unfair
represent	right	fight
traitors	cause	effect
before	after	

FIVE TRAITS OF CIVILIZATION

complex institutions	improved technology	specialized workers
record keeping	civilization	Sumer
scribes	metalworking	Catal Huyuk
surplus	hunter-gatherer	irrigation
cuneiform	trade	population
Mesopotamia	Fertile Crescent	cities
religion	teacher	government
farming	grow	laws

FIVE TRAITS OF CIVILIZATION

invent	food	production
change	cause	effect
important	develop	better
bigger	challenge	safe
reliable		

FIVE TRAITS OF CIVILIZATION

ANCIENT GREECE

city-states	Sparta and Athens	oligarchy
aristocracy	monarchy	Socrates
Acropolis	Persia	columns
polytheism	Thermopylae	Herodotus
Alexander the Great	Hippocrates	Archimedes
Homer	philosophy	polis
Salamis	war	art
democracy	Greek	United States

ANCIENT GREECE

government	300	history
math	literature	medicine
culture	isolated	independent
civilization	foundation	influence
grow	better	change
cause	effect	impact
modern	continue	start
roots		

ANCIENT GREECE

WESTWARD EXPANSION

West	East	land
slavery	Native Americans	Pacific Ocean
Great Plains	Mexico	Mississippi River
war	Texas	California
Homestead Act	Louisiana Purchase	Gold Rush
Lewis and Clark	pioneer	Transcontinental Railroad
Manifest Destiny	Oregon Trail	prospector
trapper	Conestoga	sod houses

WESTWARD EXPANSION

immigrants	Trail of Tears	free
opportunity	explore	fair
cause	effect	positive
negative		

WESTWARD EXPANSION

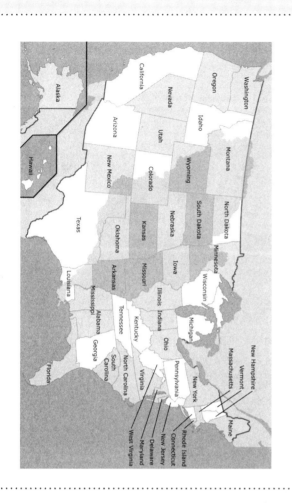

Just Try It!

Teaching is tough. I know, I know . . . #preachingtothechoir. What with constantly changing standards, hypercritical administrators, slightly insane parents, the pressure to always be "on," and the marked lack of bathroom breaks, it's a wonder any of us are still standing come June. The last thing we need—when we already feel like we are just barely treading water in the Olympic-sized pool of education—are teaching strategies that require us to attend hours of training or rework our entire curriculum . . . again. What we could really use is a strategy that is simple enough to fit in seamlessly with what we already do, yet challenges our students to think critically, making our job easier in the process.

Vocabulary Connection Cards engage students in visual, auditory, and kinesthetic learning all at the same time. They challenge students of all levels to dig deeper and see the complex nature of learning. They are flexible and naturally lend themselves to differentiation and modification. They require students to have learning conversations. They present opportunities for writing outside the ELA curriculum. They even have the potential to get parents more involved in their child's learning! They are everything a good teaching strategy should be, yet they are also incredibly simple to create and use. They even provide easy opportunities for formative assessment and data collection!

I want Vocabulary Connection Cards to be a strategy you can try on the spur of the moment without stress or extensive preparation. So next time you feel like trying something new, photocopy some of the word and picture cards from the previous chapter, or sit down and type up the first 25 to 35 words that come to mind when you think about your next unit. Print them up, cut them out, and have your students do a basic concept sort. After that, hone your word choices a bit and refer back to the table of contents. Then the next time you're in the mood, try adding in one of the extension activities, such as Teach Your Sort (page 37) or Vocabulary Link-Ups (page 39). Have 10 minutes left afterwards? Flip to Chapter 4 and try one of the writing activities. Trying something new (and impressing your administrators) doesn't have to be extra work!

I hope your experience with Vocabulary Connection Cards is as freeing as mine was, and I sincerely hope it becomes one of the most used tools in that teacher tool belt of yours! Simply write a few keywords on a few blank cards . . . and let your students make the connections!

References

Allen, J., & Landaker, C. (2005). *Reading history: A practical guide to improving literacy.* Oxford: Oxford University Press.

Ainsworth, L., & Viegut, D. (2006). *Common formative assessments: How to connect standards-based instruction and assessment.* Thousand Oaks, CA: Corwin Press.

Bear, D. R., Invernizzi, M., Templeton, S., & Johnston, F. (1996–2017). Words Their Way Series. New York: Pearson.

Bednarz, S. (2008). *World cultures and geography.* Evanston, IL: McDougal Littell.

Bitstrips Inc. (2017). Bitmoji. [computer application]. Toronto.

Bloom, B. S., Engelhart, M. D., Furst, E. J., Hill, W. H., & Krathwohl, D. R. (1956). Taxonomy of educational objectives: The classification of educational goals. *Handbook I: Cognitive domain.* New York: David McKay Company.

Brown, S. (2003). *All sorts of sorts 3: Primary, standards-based, content area vocabulary sorts in science, social studies, math, and health.* Beaverton, OR: Teaching Resource Center.

Daniels, H., Zemelman, S., & Steineke, N. (2007). *Content-area writing: Every teacher's guide.* Portsmouth, NH: Heinemann.

Everding, G. (2014, July 28). Expecting to teach enhances learning, recall | The Source | Washington University in St. Louis. Retrieved March 25, 2017, from https://source.wustl.edu/2014/07/expecting-to-teach-enhances-learning-recall/

Frayer, D., Frederick, W. C., & Klausmeier, H. J. (1969). A *schema for testing the level of cognitive mastery.* Madison, WI: Wisconsin Center for Education Research.

Gallagher, K. (2004). *Deeper reading: Comprehending challenging texts, 4–12.*
Portland, ME: Stenhouse.

Hattie, J. (2012). *Visible learning for teachers: Maximizing impact on learning.*
London: Routledge.

Hiebert, F., Thornton, C., & McInerney, J. (2016). *National geographic world history: Great civilizations ancient through early modern times.* Boston, MA: National Geographic Learning/Cengage Learning.

Marzano, R. J., Pickering, D. J., & Pollock, J. E. (2001). *Classroom instruction that works: Research-based strategies for increasing student achievement.* Alexandria, VA: Association for Supervision and Curriculum Development.

Marzano, R. J. (2004). *Building background knowledge for academic achievement: Research on what works in schools.* Alexandria, VA: ASCD.

Mendler, D. A. (2013, November 5). Teaching your students how to have a conversation. Retrieved March 25, 2017, from https://www.edutopia.org/blog/teaching-your-students-conversation-allen-mendler

National Governors Association Center for Best Practices & Council of Chief State School Officers. (2010). *Common core state standards.* Washington, DC.

Santa, C. M. (1988). *Content reading including study systems: Reading, writing and studying across the curriculum.* Dubuque, IA: Kendall Hunt Publishing

Stiggins, R. J., Arter, J. A., Chappuis, J., & Chappuis, S. (2007). *Classroom assessment for student learning: Doing it right — using it well.* Upper Saddle River, NJ: Pearson Education, Inc.

Templeton, S., Bear, D. R., Invernizzi, M., Johnston, F. R., Flanigan, K., Townsend, D. R., Helman, L., & Hayes, L. (2015). *Vocabulary their way: Word study with middle and secondary students.* Upper Saddle River, NJ: Pearson Education.

Valentine, J. (2005, August). The instructional practices inventor: A process for profiling student engaged learning for school improvement. Retrieved June 20, 2017, from http://mllc.missouri.edu/Upload%20Area-Docs/IPI%20Manuscript%208-05.pdf

Photo Credits